CW00518266

Col

❖   ❖   ❖

Thanks to . . .
My rock and wife Gemma; my most wonderful daughters
Amylia and Alanya; my mum and dad who made me the
person I am today; Brian Whelan for making this book
possible; Dr Roberts and all the staff at Torbay Hospital; all
sponsors who made the original book's publication possible;
John Hartson for the book's foreword; Swansea City;
Drogheda United; Exeter City; Torquay United; Salisbury
City; Newport County; Forest Green Rovers; all of the clubs'
supporters; The History Press for the new edition.
If I have left someone out then I am truly sorry.
I really do appreciate everyone's help and support.

❖   ❖   ❖

Foreword

by John Hartson

Ifirst met Chris Todd at Newport County's training ground in 2010. I'd been asked by their then CEO/caretaker manager Tim Harris to help out with training. I had been aware of Chris from a young age as I was an avid Swansea fan. He happened to play in the same team as my brother-in-law and I would therefore follow their results religiously. Chris went on to play over 50 games in the first team at Swansea before joining Drogheda United in the Republic of Ireland, Exeter City, Torquay United and then on to Newport County.

I remember watching Chris train and commenting on his attitude and how keen he was – and how impressed I was with his overall approach to the game. He would listen and take on board all that I said.

It was only then that we got to know each other and I learned that in November 2008 at the age of 27 Chris had been diagnosed with Chronic Myeloid Leukaemia, a form of cancer in the blood. When Chris explained what he had been through and the treatment and chemotherapy he had received I was shocked. In front of me I saw a big, strong lad, a picture of health and to think that he had put up such a fight and shown great courage to return to the game was amazing. I was so impressed and had the utmost respect for him. I too had been touched by cancer in July 2009 so I felt that immediately we had a strong bond as we both had fought and beaten such a killer of a disease.

What some don't realise is that when you have the displeasure of going through chemotherapy, it not only knocks the stuffing out of you but you are in a tremendous amount of pain and find it hard to cope with general life and day-to-day worries. The fact that Chris fought this illness head-on and was back playing in such a short space of time deserves the highest admiration. What an achievement.

Chris took 6 months out to undergo chemotherapy and treatment for CML and within that time he successfully beat the illness and was in remission. After Chris underwent treatment, he had a loan spell at Salisbury before returning to Torquay for the last month of the 2008/09 season. He went straight back into the first team and returned to the pitch in style by playing in the Conference Premier play-off final at Wembley against Cambridge United and, during this month, he won the 'Man of the Match' and helped Torquay win the game and promotion to League Two. This would have been the second time Chris was involved in promotion – I remember watching Swansea City promoted from the then Division 3 to Division 2 under John Hollins back in 2000.

Also like me, Chris had the full support of his family. He is one of four brothers along with Liam, Thomas and James. James is a boxer who is presently looking for a promoter to further his career. When you are fighting an illness like this, it takes over yours and your family's life and you start to put in perspective how much you mean to each other. I was told that Chris's brothers were by his side every step of the way.

Chris released the first edition of this book back in 2011. He wrote and published the book himself to raise money for Leukaemia & Lymphoma Research. Speaking from experience, writing a book is a very difficult thing to do. While writing mine, I found I visited some dark times. You start reminiscing and going over things and past events in your life. Chris has done so well to give such a clear outlook to what he went through and it must be so encouraging for leukaemia sufferers.

I would like to wish Chris all the best for his future with his wife Gemma and two young daughters. He is a great lad and a good character both on and off the pitch. I hope he does well at Forest Green and has a few playing years left in him.

Our biggest battle may have been beating cancer but being healthy, in remission and looking forward to what life has in store is something we've both got in common and something we both have got to be very grateful for every single day.

Best wishes
John Hartson, 2012

LEUKAEMIA & LYMPHOMA RESEARCH

Beating Blood Cancers

Chris Todd was diagnosed with chronic myeloid leukaemia – a type of blood cancer – and survived.

Chris is one of the lucky ones. Around 30,000 people are diagnosed with a blood cancer in the UK every year, and sadly one person every hour dies from the disease.

Leukaemia & Lymphoma Research is the only UK charity solely dedicated to research into all the types of blood cancer including leukaemia, lymphoma and myeloma. Research and clinical trials are vital to improving treatments and saving lives.

With your support we can achieve our aim of beating blood cancer. To find out more, visit ✆ beatingbloodcancers.org.uk or call ☎ 020 7405 0101

The Diary

My week started no different to any of the previous weeks. I was fighting back from a groin injury I had sustained against Forest Green in late September. It was a problem that had started just weeks into the start of the season, but I was managing to look after it and get through games. I thought I had a Gilmore's groin, which involves a tear of the abductor muscles, usually high up near the attachment to the pubic bone. In most cases it can be managed and it is a common injury in footballers throughout their careers, purely down to wear and tear. The best way to describe it is as if someone is hanging on the lower half of your body and won't let go. A few months into the league it was really taking its toll on me, but I wouldn't give in until late September. I was up early in the morning, had my breakfast, and headed in for training.

For some reason I decided to ring the club doctor and asked him to do a blood test on me after training. I hadn't been feeling the best, and had been coming home from training feeling totally fatigued. It was only today on my way to training that I started to feel a bit faint – it was as if I had no strength in my body and it felt as if it wanted to shut down. So putting two and two together I thought that I should ring the doctor, and ask him if he could do the blood test. When I had my groin operation a few weeks previously a nurse told me to get one, as she was concerned that I was bleeding more than normal when she removed the needle.

Training was fast and furious, and I was working hard with our exceptional physio Damian Davey. Then, after finishing my session with him, I asked if I could join in with the youth team for a five-a-side game, as I had not trained properly for over a month. I was running about like an idiot, knocking about and throwing my body here, there, and everywhere, as I would normally have done. I was just glad that I was involved in some form of physical contact, yet I didn't know how serious it all could have been. And then I went into the doctor and had a right laugh and joke about getting my blood done. I have no fear of needles as I have lots of tattoos – in fact, eight in total. After having the test I went home to the family for the night, to relax, and watch television.

Later that night I was sitting there with my missus, Gemma, and my little princess Amylia, watching *I'm a Celebrity, Get Me Out of Here!* – sad, I know, but that's the glamour of a footballer's life – when my phone rang. It was Raith Gwinnet, one of the club's young players saying that the doctor was at his house, the Club Lodge (this is a club house where the young players live when they move away from home. It's a house with lots of rooms and has a digs lady who looks after them like a second mum), waiting to speak to me.

After the usual pleasantries were exchanged I prepared myself for some advice about my groin injury. I didn't know it at the time, but that phone call would change my life forever. The doctor proceeded to tell me the most earth-shattering news I ever received in my life –

the blood tests had come back with the result that I had leukaemia, and would have to go to the hospital the very next morning.

What a bombshell – today was the best I had felt in ages. Luckily Gemma was right next to me, and could hear everything. So there I was coming off the phone, breaking down, and wondering what the hell was happening, thinking about how I was ever going to tell my close family and friends that I had this illness. I suppose I was thinking more about them than I was about myself. I only ever thought that young children got leukaemia. I had been so healthy all of my life except for the routine footballer's injuries. All sorts of thoughts were going through my head. How could a killer disease strike me down in the prime of my life when I had always taken such good care of my health? This was going to be the hardest challenge I had ever been forced to face. Later on that night, Chris Hargreaves (Greavsey), the Torquay United club captain, rang for a chat, and I told him the news. There was silence on the other end of the phone. Within hours my family were down the M4 like a shot. Tomorrow is going to be the start of the biggest fight of my life.

18/11/08 – Is it True?

Having been told the news the previous day it still feels unreal. I'm a young, fit footballer – surely the diagnosis is wrong? I feel fit and healthy. The news only hit home earlier when I saw mum in the garden in floods of tears, in a terrible state of shock and distress. Then all of a sudden my dad popped out of my living room. We just stared at each other and smiled. Then the emotion got to both of us. He grabbed me so hard, I grabbed him back, and we didn't move for what felt like a lifetime. This was something we hadn't done for years, as we have other ways of showing our love. Then my mum came back into the house, broke down, and began cuddling me. So there we all were crying, yet at the same time all trying to be as strong as possible. I went upstairs, to get changed ready to go to the hospital, when my eldest brother Liam came out of one of the bedrooms, and as brothers do he just said, 'Are you OK, bro?' I could see he was hurting, but he is my big brother, and was going to be strong. So a deep breath and off I went to do battle.

It was like a road trip, with my missus, daughter, mum, dad, brother and Damian Davey, all joining me. We got to the hospital and I still didn't know what to think. I signed in and waited for the call to come. When it came I went into what looked like a dentist's room (there was even a chair like you'd find there). To ease the tension I cracked a joke (as you do), but the doctor didn't find it funny.

'Toddy, sit down and shut up,' I thought, as he told us the news. You could have heard a pin drop. There was a stunned silence, but the silence was broken by the doctor continuing to speak, my mum and missus sobbing, and Amylia making noises – too young to understand what was happening. He told me that I had Chronic Myeloid Leukaemia (CML), explained what it was, how it could be treated, and then asked me if I wanted to go home and take things in. I replied 'no', and asked if I could start the treatment right away. I wasn't trying to be a hero, but thought to myself, 'let's start the fight'. I had more blood tests, and also a bone marrow test, which was a rather strange feeling as it feels like someone is drilling into your back, and then you get this big popping feeling when the bone marrow comes out.

A bone marrow test is to see whether there are cancer cells present. For this test, the doctor removes a tiny sample of bone marrow cells to look at under the microscope. These tests are largely done for cancers which are most likely to affect the bone marrow, such as lymphomas, myeloma and, of course my illness, leukaemia. But it can be done for any type of cancer, if your doctor thinks your bone marrow could contain cancer cells, or needs to rule it out for any reason.

When we got home my other two brothers had arrived (Thomas and James). Both of them were in bits, and wanted to know everything. I explained the story to them, and I don't know if they understood, but they tried to take it all in. That night they wanted to do something nice for me, so went on the internet and looked for 'livestrong' bands, which they could wear on their wrists to show their support and solidarity. I found this a nice touch . . . until they asked me to pay for them.

They have hearts of gold but as they said themselves, 'big brothers always pay'. It had been a long day, but that wasn't the end of it. Torquay were playing Lewes in an important league match, putting a 14-game unbeaten run on the line, and I decided that I was going to go as normal. Paul Buckle (the Torquay manager) and Chris Hargeaves were the first people to know from the club, and they asked me how I wanted the rest of the lads to find out. I asked if I could tell them myself, which they agreed to. It was one of the hardest things I have ever done, especially standing there watching grown men cry. I stayed strong, as I wanted to tell them everything, even some of the scientific stuff, which isn't my strong point. On the way out, they all shook my hand and I could see that they felt so many different things but they were right behind me. When they had all left it was me, my dad, the club doctor Andy Ryan, and Brian Paulk (a club director). My dad grabbed me, was in tears again, and whispered 'Cry – you're allowed to'. So that's what I did

– and it felt good. It was so hard telling my team-mates, although they're much more than that to me. They're my sporting family. My friends.

The lads went on to win 4–1, and when Tim Sills scored the first goal early in the game, the lads ran to the dugout, got my shirt (number 6, the number I have tried to have at every club I've played at), and held it up, in respect and support, which touched me greatly. It was funny as well, as a fan sitting behind me said that they must have been doing it to wind me up, as I wasn't playing. He just didn't have a clue what was going on!

We are a very close squad, and I know people will say 'Oh, we've heard that many times before', but the team spirit at this club is incredible. We are a family, and that includes the players, management and staff. We all have a special bond.

19/11/08 – Press Conference

I had to go down to Torquay's ground to do a press conference to let the public know about my illness, but most importantly how determined I was to fight it. My parents, Steve and Julie, Gemma and Amylia, Alex Rowe (chairman), Colin Lee (CEO), Paul Buckle (club manager) and Greavsey were all there. I knew how much support they were going to give me which was incredibly touching.

The whole press conference was surreal. It was like a scene out of the Premiership, so I cracked a joke telling the gaffer that this whole thing was really about me joining Manchester United, which gave him a good laugh. Colin spoke first, outlining that I had been diagnosed with CML. When it was my turn to speak I started with a bit of humour, saying 'Obviously it's a bit of bad news for me!' In my whole career I have never done as many interviews. I told mum and dad that I should record myself, and just play it every time someone was interviewing me.

Looking back it's like a jigsaw puzzle – you remember things that you couldn't understand at the time. I was struggling to keep up with the lads in pre-season. I'm a pretty good athlete and was always at the top of the bunch, and I couldn't understand why I was behind them all the time. I guess I just thought that I had too good an off season!

I know I have had upsets in my career and this is just another one – I will deal with it, and will be back. I've had many setbacks in my career that have made me a better player and a stronger person. I've got to tell you about four of the worst games I have been involved in:

Lincoln v Swansea

With only a few full league games under my belt everything had been going so well up until this one. I played by far my worst 10 minutes of football at Sincil Bank. It was going well for the first 35 minutes, then I gave a needless foul away just outside the box and Tony Thorpe decided to step up and blast it into the back of the net. 1–0 down. Then, as if that wasn't bad enough, within a couple of minutes I hit a short back-pass that went totally wrong and their winger latched onto it and all of a sudden it's 2–0. By this time I wanted to be swallowed up by the ground. At the end of the game we had lost 2–0 and it was all my fault. It was a hard lesson to learn so early in my career. It was by far my worst half of football in a Swansea shirt!

Cardiff v Swansea (FAW Premier Cup final, May 2002)

This was my first chance to play in a Cardiff derby, and being a local lad it was something I had always dreamed of – playing against our biggest rivals. It was coming to the end of the season and my contract was coming to an end. I wanted so badly to play, then manager Nick Cusack dropped me and stuck me on the bench! Little did I know that was to be the beginning of the end of my Swansea career. I was an unused sub in a 1–0 defeat to a Graham Kavanagh goal. It always disappoints me to think that I never got the chance to play in a Jack–Bluebird derby.

Exeter v Morecambe (play-off final, May 2007)

To captain a team at Wembley was my boyhood dream, but to lose there as captain and have to walk up those great stairs was a nightmare. We went 1–0 up with a Lee Phillips goal and everything was rosy. I even gave a penalty away that Paul Jones saved from Wayne Curtis to spare my blushes. Then, just when we thought our name was on the cup, 3 minutes before half time we lost a goal because of some sloppy defending. After the break the game became a cagey affair with nothing much happening. It looked like we would be heading for extra time, until, on the 82nd minute, a long, hoofed clearance produced a wonder goal by Danny Carlton that killed 30,000 Grecian fans' dreams (and my own).

Torquay Utd v Ebbsfleet (FA Trophy final, May 2008)

Wembley again and another bad day. This time I was the man at fault for a lapse of concentration in our 1–0 defeat. A minute before half time a ball played down the line where I was covering looked to be running out of play on Wembley's lush turf – well that's what I thought! The ball decided to hold up just before the line and their striker Jon Akinde robbed me of the ball and crossed it to Chris McPhee (who had missed a penalty earlier)to do the rest. I felt sick and couldn't believe my bad luck.

To this day I wish I had not trusted the lush surface and just booted it into the thousands of fans, but hey, that's football.

20/11/08 – Back Training

I was determined to get on with life as normal, so this morning I went off to training as per usual. It was just the injured lads there, so I went for a run with two of them: Wayne Carlisle and Nicky Wroe. It started off as a small run, but after a while the lads started to kick on, moving away from me. I shouted after them, 'For God's sake, lads! Any chance of slowing down? I've got leukaemia, remember?' They turned around and didn't know what to say, not sure if I was serious or not. But I just fell about the place laughing, as did they. Wayne then roared back, 'I'm not giving you any advantages, I want you back playing.' After the run the lads went in, and Damian and myself played a game of head-tennis, which I won. It was close as he's still got a bit about him, but if he had won I would have retired.

Afterwards I told Damian that I needed to do something, and so I started shouting as loud as I could to try to relieve all the pain inside me. It was loud (I am Welsh after all), and it felt good.

A great support to me has been my team-mate and friend Chris Hargreaves. 'Greavesy' is one of my best friends. Let's just say he looks like a good-looking Frank Gallagher from the television show Shameless. The two of us were Paul Buckle's first two signings when he took over. When I first saw him I thought to myself, 'Who is this flash foreign guy?', but then he opened his mouth and I soon realised that he was a witty northerner who had picked up a few bits of slang on his football travels. It's ironic really, as soon after chatting to him I realised that we had a lot of shared history. We had both appeared in the play-off semi-final just a year earlier in a dramatic 4–3 Exeter City win over Oxford, where we both captained each team, me being on the happier side (Exeter). When we chatted some more I found out that I had played against him when I made my debut as a 19-year-old for Swansea against Northampton in a 1–1 draw. From that day we hit it off, becoming great car buddies, roomies and most importantly, great friends.

Chris later became Torquay's captain, and is someone who, as a player, I have so much respect for, even though his banter is as dry as it comes. How could I not? The guy is a natural winner, a true football gladiator with a great football pedigree, and to still be playing at his age in the shape he is in is a credit to the man. Given the chance, one day he will make a great manager. Oh, by the way, I am still alive and kicking.

21/11/08 – Fighting Back

Did a few weights in the gym, went for a quick jog, then had a game of head-tennis with Wayne Carlisle that I lost 2–1. We were playing Woking in a massive game; our form was good but a lot of teams were playing well. That night we got to the hotel where we had an evening meal together before all the lads went to bed. Yes, the Friday nights away generally consist of a big feed, and then an early night. But the gaffer told the two of us that we could go off for a drink if we fancied it. There was a little pub around the corner where we had a few pints of the 'black stuff', and got chatting to a few people who were also staying in our hotel. They were salesmen, so a bit full of it, as you can imagine. One of them cracked jokes all night long, which was something that I really needed. This is one of them, although it is rather cheesy. A polar bear walked into a bar, goes up to the barmaid and says, 'Can I get a pint offffffff . . . Fosters please?' The barmaid then replies, 'Why the big pause?' The polar bear then says, 'I'm a polar bear'.

22/11/08 – Bike Racing

This morning I went for a run with Damian and the other injured players, before returning to the ground for the pre-match meal. When everyone had finished we travelled the short distance to Woking's ground for a crucial league match. This really was an emotional time for me. Bucks asked me to lead the team out, which was an absolute honour. The way the fans reacted to me – clapping, chanting my name, holding up 'Get Well Soon' signs, etc. – really got to me. The game didn't start too well as we went behind 2–0 after only 22 minutes. Woking were really fired-up, but after a half-time chat we showed real fighting spirit to draw 2–2, courtesy of goals from Elliot Benyon and Danny Stevens. The spirit is really beginning to show right through the club, and that's now 16 games unbeaten for us.

After the game we went back to the hotel to get changed – I thought I looked amazing until the lads started ripping into me about my shirt, saying I looked either like a WWE referee or a gangster – they weren't sure which one. I think they really liked it, and that's why they had such a go at it. Don't ask me why lads do that – it's just a man thing, and then they generally go off a week later and buy one for themselves.

So off we went to London, and who did we meet? Only Phil Mitchell from Eastenders! The night's highlight was when we went bike-racing around the streets, screaming at the bikers to go faster as we raced each other. When it was finished Robbo and myself gave our drivers £10 each – a good effort from two Celts to part with money so easily! Then we realised that two of the lads had decided to do a runner without paying, and when we caught up with them we realised that we were being chased. We eventually made it to a pizza place, and then we started wondering why we were running considering we had paid – shows the bond team-mates have I guess. One of the bikers was still chasing after us shouting, 'I want my money!' He gave up after 30 minutes – I think he needed to keep his energy for the next race.

When I got home to Devon I looked back on the weekend. We got a good point at Woking (and perhaps should have got all three), and had an eventful time with the lads. It was just what I needed, as it took my mind off the leukaemia. Thanks lads.

24/11/08 – Early Results

Today my parents were back down as they knew I was going back to the hospital to find out how far I was in CML terms after having all my tests last week. It was going to be tough, as I honestly didn't have any inclination as to what news they would have for me. I was in a positive frame of mind and was convinced it would be good news. They sat us down and got straight to the point, 'Well, Mr Todd, do you remember when I said to you last week that you would need a certain gene in your bone marrow if you were going to be able to take the tablets to try to calm your CML down? Well I'm delighted to say that you do have it.' What this meant was that I would have to take one tablet a day (forever

I hoped). There may come a day when I may need the more severe chemotherapy, but fingers crossed I won't, and at the moment this news is a silver lining.

There are so many different side-effects to this drug – one being gout – so for the first 2 months I would have to take a double dosage to try to prevent this. If you actually sit down and read the leaflet that comes with something as simple as paracetamol, or aspirin, you wouldn't take them for fear of the side-effects. So I hope when I start, that I don't suffer any of these. Only time will tell I guess.

We have also discussed fertility, which thankfully isn't a major downside, and we're going to save some of my sperm just to be sure in the future. The doctor said she would sort me out for an appointment in the sperm clinic, probably on Thursday. Once I do that I can start taking my tablets on Saturday. Today was as good as I could have hoped for – it was nice to have at least a little bit of good news.

25/11/08 – Positive

Today I woke up in an even more positive mood than previously, knowing the aims and targets that were ahead for me. So I went to training and decided to tell the lads the news. We have a circle when someone's got good or bad news, and lately it's been bad, so I thought to myself 'let's give them some half-decent news today'. The reaction was great when I told them about the news from the hospital.

I didn't leave it at that though – I also told them about my impending visit to the sperm bank. They loved it, and I told them that it was going to be like a scene out of the film *American Pie* – watch this space.

26/11/08 – Visit

Well I was very nervous today as I went off to Plymouth for my visit to the sperm bank. After hours of driving I couldn't find the place so went around asking people for directions to it. Needless to say I got some funny looks. I eventually found it, walked in, went up the lift to the sixth floor, walked through the doors and into reception. So there I was standing at the desk asking the lady behind it if I was in the right place and what to do next. Then I turned around and saw all the people in the waiting room. The place was packed! At the top of my voice I said, 'Hi, my name's Chris Todd; I'm here to give some sperm.' Then I just sat down and could see everyone staring at me – haha! After about a quarter of an hour I got the call, and off I went following this nurse who took me into a room where I had to fill in an incredible amount of forms. Then the nurse said to me, 'Are you ready?' Off I went into another room – a shockingly small, sleazy room. Before the nurse left she turned to me and said, 'If you need any help, the magazines are in the top drawer,' and then she locked the door behind her. I couldn't stop laughing. The whole situation was surreal. Sure, I had to have a look through the magazines which turned out to be throwbacks to the 1970s! Anyway, I did the business, gave my sperm, and hoped there was enough. Then it was a quick escape to the car, and off home. Job done!

That night my eldest brother and his missus came down with my nephew Charlie. I told him about my day, which naturally enough he thought was hilarious. Then it got worse as I got a call from the hospital – 'Mr Todd, we have your specimen . . . but there's not enough.' I couldn't believe it! So you can imagine the stick I got off everyone over that one! With my male pride hurt I asked if I could go back down tomorrow but was told, 'You'd best rest tomorrow, and come back Friday.' Thanks, I really needed to hear that. . . .

27/11/08 – American Pie

On the way into training all I was thinking about was how I was going to tell the boys what had happened. When I told them they were falling about laughing – as you can imagine. When I said it was like a scene out of *American Pie*, they loved it. On a serious note, I spoke to Damian about sorting out some vitamins and proteins to help me with what was ahead (and no, it's not for the return visit to the sperm bank!).

When I signed for Torquay and found out that Damian Davey was also there I was an extremely happy man. I had worked with him at Exeter City and knew what he was about – at least I thought I did. I always knew that he was a great physio, and a funny one at that. They always say that you have to heal the mind before you heal the person and Damian had that off to a tee. He has got a story for just about everything and if you're feeling a bit down after a game, or have something personal on your mind, Damo's physio room is the place to be. You would often see half the squad in there – he really is like a male 'Dear Deirdre'.

When I told him the news of my illness I wasn't quite sure how he would react, but he was devastated. I never knew how much he cared about the players and he stupidly blamed himself for what had happened to me. That was crazy. I knew how much he tried to prevent injuries, and that all the players depended on him to 'fix' us. But this time it really was out of his hands. Then again he has become a guardian angel to me and has never left my side. He has really seen my ups and downs, having been to the doctor, or just having a bad day at training.

28/11/08 – Return Visit

I made it back to the sperm bank today – hopefully for the last time. This time there were no forms – it was just straight into the room and I was ready to do it. I went in and finished what I needed to do – and yes, I did look at the 1970s throwbacks again, these magazines are getting better! Anyway, I grabbed my cup to check how full it was, held it up to the light, and shook it to make sure there was enough in it this time. Then the worst thing possible happened. I spilled it everywhere. What a disaster! What a mess! It was turning into a nightmare, and I had no more days left to return as I start taking my tablets tomorrow, so this was the last chance. I sat there for a while and then cleaned up the mess. It had now definitely turned into a scene out of American Pie. The nurse came up to me with a big smiley face on her and said, 'Finished?' I didn't know whether to laugh or cry. 'Sorry, there's been an accident,' I said, 'a spillage.' She looked at me like she wanted to laugh her head off, but she tried to be professional and went to get somebody else. I think she just needed to breathe before bursting with laughter. Another nurse came in and thankfully said, 'Well I think we have just got enough here.' Thank God for that. I walked out of the place the other day at a rapid pace, but you'd swear I was in the Olympic 100-metre race the speed I left at today.

They say life is like a rollercoaster, and they're right. What a week! I'm learning so much about life it's untrue . . . and it's only just started.

I was lucky enough to speak to Geoff Thomas (an ex-England international footballer who in the past has had the same illness as me) because Wayne Carlisle of Exeter City passed my number over to him through a friend of Geoff's and told him what had happened to me.

When Wayne told me that Geoff might ring me I never got my hopes up, mainly owing to the fact that I thought he would have other worries and commitments. How wrong was I? He took it upon himself to ring me, and it really was a surprise. I wasn't quite sure if it was him at first. We talked for a while and I soon realised that it was the man himself. He was such a breath of fresh air as he was so positive. We talked about the illness and how I was really feeling. When I told him, he said that I sounded so positive about it all and that was the start I needed. He asked me about my side-effects and when I told him about my legs he explained that he had the exact same thing and not to worry about it. He finished the call by saying that if I ever wanted to chat about anything then to simply pick up the phone. The call was a big lift and I'll never forget it.

Geoff also inspired me due to the work he did through his foundation. With all the publicity that my illness has attracted, I think it's only right that I can give something back to the people who have helped me. To that end I want to encourage you to visit the Anthony Nolan Trust website, and consider getting yourself on the bone marrow register. It's pretty simple. It's basically a blood test, with the trust sending you a couple of tubes that you take with you to your GP. The doctor takes the blood, fills in some forms, and you send it in. It's simple enough and it could save somebody's life.

29/11/08 – Well Wishes

Last night has been the toughest yet since my diagnosis. Amylia was up all night with teething problems, and Gemma was ill with a bad stomach. She has been sick for a while now, which is a bit worrying for me as if I catch it, it will be ten times worse. So I am the domestic housewife for the next few days while she is confined to the bedroom . . . and not for the right reasons!

Today was our meeting with Oxford United in the FA Cup, and was the first home game we have had since the news about my illness came out. My parents came down as per usual to show their support. I was aching and very tired when I arrived at the ground, but the support I received when I got there was heartening (I have already received hundreds of cards, messages, and get well gestures). Supporters were coming up to me and shaking my hand, taking photographs and wishing me well. I don't think I have ever had so many cuddles and kisses from people I didn't know.

I went into the dressing room before the match to catch up with the lads, and as soon as I walked through the door they asked me how it went at the sperm bank. Needless to say they fell about the place laughing again. See, I can still do my bit for the team – they were buzzing! Elliot Benyon got the goals for us today (two good finishes) in a 2–0 win, and we are now through to the third round of the FA Cup.

At half time I went onto the pitch to do the draw and what a reception I received – it was amazing – so I said a few words of thanks which made the crowd go crazy, and I felt on top of the world. I needed that boost today. The cup is something players and directors at our level dream of, hopefully drawing one of the big clubs out of the hat. So come on Arsenal or Swansea! When I was at Exeter we played Manchester United away in front of 60,000 people. I was injured though . . . how's that for bad luck? The money from playing them was the foundation for the last couple of seasons of success Exeter have achieved.

When I got home I took my first tablet – the first of many. It was a strange feeling, as I knew that this would be me for the rest of my days, but sometimes a man's gotta do, what a man's gotta do.

30/11/08 – Watching Soccer

I felt great today so went for a 20-minute run, and felt good after it. Two great games on the box today, with the big Welsh derby between Swansea (come on you Jacks) and Cardiff, and the London derby between Arsenal and Chelsea. The results weren't too bad with Swansea drawing 2–2, and Arsenal winning 2–1.

I started feeling unwell today, having a bad stomach, which I think I caught from Gemma. I was wondering when that was going to happen, as I'm going to catch things more easily now. I really feel that I'm being tested. I've only just started my treatment and I'm bad already. Let's just say this – it can only get better, I hope.

1/12/08 – Matchstick Man

I've had a really bad night, and have been on the toilet for most of it. My stomach is churning, and I didn't get much sleep at all, so no training for me today. I've been on the phone to the hospital and they advised me to take it easy, and drink lots of water, which will be hard. If the way I'm feeling continues, and I get a temperature I will have to go back to the hospital. I am sitting here trying not to feel sorry for myself but it's difficult. I've lost so much weight, and if it carries on I'm going to look like a matchstick man. I have never been a thick-set lad – I weigh in at approximately 79–80kgs. I have always found it hard to put on weight over the years. I have tried all sorts of weight programmes and supplement drinks to try to affect it. I do believe my frame could easily carry another stone. It's not that I don't try to eat – I eat like a horse! Guess I'm just meant to be a lean, mean, fighting machine.

I took a rest earlier, finally got some sleep, and am feeling a lot better. My stomach has finally stopped churning and it is a relief not to feel like shit. To be fair, the hospital has been great to me. They must be thinking, 'this guy's only started taking tablets 3 days ago, and he hasn't stopped ringing us'. They did say to ring if anything was wrong but they probably didn't expect it would only take 2 days! They really are amazing people, doing an incredibly difficult job.

2/12/08 – Bad Stomach

Today has been another bad day when it comes to my stomach. Woke up, felt OK, and then all of a sudden my stomach went a bit 'mad' to say the very least, and I was stuck to the toilet again – me and the toilet have a very special bond at the moment. I wish I had a TV in there. I did manage to keep some food down, which made me feel a bit better. It's mad to think how much weight you lose, and how weak you feel when you miss a few days' food. It makes you think how poorer countries have to cope with disease and a lack of food.

On a football note I missed training again, which is really killing me. If it carries on I'm going to have to just grin and bear it, and run with a nappy on, or maybe borrow one from Amylia.

Today was supposed to be my comeback game against Forest Green in the Setanta Shield (we lost 1–0), following my groin operation. Well that return is obviously on hold at the moment but going through what I'm going through, I'm more determined than ever to get back on that field again.

3/12/08 – Better

Today has been the best day I've had since I've been ill. I had a bad night again last night but I'm going to try not to moan, as that's all I've been doing really. You've got to feel sorry for my missus and her sister, who is now living with us, for having to listen to me. It must have sounded like a jungle in my toilet for the last few days. Hopefully when I take my tablet later I'll be OK.

We put up the Christmas tree tonight. I love Christmas, always have done since I was a child. It's the best time of the year – who wouldn't want to spend quality time with their family?

4/12/08 – Good Morning

My stomach has calmed down and I've finally got my appetite back. I went back into training, as I was feeling better, so cracked on with the weights as normal, messing around with the lads and generally just having a laugh. Like I have done frequently, I went for a run with Damian, who really is proving to be a brilliant help as he is so positive. After that I joined in with the lads for the finishing session, as I was feeling good. I really did have my shooting boots on and was hitting the target from all over (the lads were asking for some of my tablets as they were obviously working!). It felt good to be hitting the leather out of the ball again after so long. I wished the lads all the best for Saturday as I am heading to London with Gemma, so won't be at the game. It's going to be nice to spend some quality time with each other, shopping, sightseeing, romantic walks, etc. Oh, and just in case you thought I was getting soppy, we're also going to a boxing match – well, you've got to do some man's stuff!

5/12/08 – Early Start

We had an early start today as we had to drive from Devon to Swansea, to catch the 6.00 a.m. bus to London as we were going away for the weekend. A long old journey, 5 hours in total, but I slept all the way through it! When we got there we went to the nearest tube station and got the all-day 'Hopper Pass' for £5.30. The ticket was well used that's for sure, as we were going here, there and everywhere by mistake sometimes. We visited the London Dungeon, the London Eye and Buckingham Palace – all the things tourists do. We walked our feet off, and even though I'm missing training these days, I know my fitness isn't, and won't be, a problem.

6/12/08 – Walking

I had a really good night's sleep (for a change), and woke up ready for another day's walking. We went to Camden Market, which was amazing – just up Gemma's street. We bartered and haggled all day which was really good fun. When we went round the shops it was a nightmare trying to get in and out of them, being pushed and shoved about. Thankfully this isn't a regular occurrence for me as my Saturdays are normally spent playing football.

That night we went to the pub for food, and it was the first time I had to take my tablet while out, so if anyone was watching me they probably thought I was some sort of a junkie. Later we went to see Enzo Maccarinelli take on Matthew Ellis at the ExCel Arena – he beat him inside two rounds. Afterwards we went to the after-party where we got to meet a few other famous boxers, as well as Danny from the band McFly.

My 20-year old brother James has recently turned professional, and trains in the same gym in Newbridge as Enzo, as well as Joe Calzaghe, and is guided by Joe's father Enzo (James has been in the Calzaghe camp for some time). James' first professional fight is coming up soon in Bristol, and I'm really nervous about it.

Even though I've been visiting many doctors, going to the hospital and waiting for test results over the past few weeks, I'm more nervous about the fight to be honest. I don't know much about James' opponent other than that he's also making his first professional bow. If I could describe James' boxing style in one word, it would be that he's a brawler. I don't think amateur boxing really suited him as a result of that but now hopefully the world of professional boxing will suit him better.

I spoke to many members of the Calzaghe camp after the fight, and they're all so supportive of me, and what I'm going through. I spoke to Maccarinelli and he told me that he's trying to organise some sort of a charity football match to raise funds for Cancer Research, featuring the likes of Calzaghe and Ricky Hatton. We might even get to play it at the Liberty Stadium in Swansea. I couldn't believe it so asked him if he was serious to which he replied that they'd all love to do it . . . so we'll see what happens. If it does it will be brilliant.

7/12/08 – Shattered

On Sunday morning I had a great breakfast on my tod, as Gemma was too lazy to get up. In fairness I was shattered myself but when she did eventually get up we went for a romantic stroll through Hyde Park, before heading home. I wasn't looking forward to the drive as I have long legs, and find it hard to get comfortable, but Gemma is a short-arse and could sleep in a carrier bag.

In 2003 I signed for League of Ireland side Drogheda United, a club which had a mix of both full-time and part-time footballers. It was only a short-term deal but really was a wonderful experience. It would appear that I was fondly remembered by some supporters there as a few years ago I was interviewed for the club's matchday programme, and then shortly after for a book called *DUFC: A Claret and Blue History*, written by one of the club's supporters, Brian Whelan, about the history of the club. During the course of the interview Brian asked me if I knew that my name had achieved cult status, to which I obviously replied 'no'. He told me that one of the club's supporters was moaning on an online forum that he was sitting in a bar on his own, but instead of saying he was on his own he said that he was 'on his Chris Todd'. This phrase has since stuck for some of the supporters, who still use it today in everyday conversation. I'm sure they get some funny looks.

8/12/08 – Second Home

I had to go to the hospital at 9.30 this morning for some more blood tests. It makes me laugh every time I go in and get a ticket with a number on it. You're called in, a quick needle, and you're done. It's as if you're going in to buy meat from Tesco.

Later, after going running with Damian, I managed to get in some long-range passing with Shaun North. I was like Becks . . . well at least I thought I was. I was finding pass after pass; maybe these tablets have superpowers that I wasn't aware of? When training was finished I went back to my second home, Torbay Hospital, for my results. They had just started a new system there so I was warned that I might be waiting longer than usual, and they were right. The results were not great, but again not too bad. The doctor seemed to think it was because of the bug I had suffered at the start of the week. So fingers crossed I won't pick up any more bugs this week, I'll get a full dose of the drugs and see an improvement next time.

9/12/08 – Listening to the Radio

I was so lazy today, but it's nice to have a 'me day' sometimes. I had no training today as the lads are away – they left yesterday afternoon for the game against Eastbourne. I couldn't go, though, as I had to go to the hospital for more check-ups. I'll be listening on the radio tonight, with my fingers crossed hoping for a good result. As I'm writing this Amylia is watching *Spongebob Squarepants* on the TV. Don't ask me why, but she loves it. She's not well at the moment, but is my world, and makes me smile every day. Bet I catch her cold though . . . these bugs are following me around at the moment.

10/12/08 – Pieces

No training again today as the lads didn't get back until the early hours of the morning. We lost to Eastbourne last night, and we're all gutted with that result. It just goes to show how hard the league is, though. It's of a very high standard with lots of clubs pumping money into their squads to get back into the Football League. Teams like Oxford, Wrexham, Mansfield and Cambridge are just some of those pushing at the top, and some of the budgets are incredible. There are rumours of one club having a squad budget of up to £1m and I'd bet you that isn't far off being the truth. There's always a dark horse, a team that comes from nowhere. This year it's Histon, the part-time outfit who have set the league on fire. The season is really hitting its peak. The thing that makes this league so good is the inconsistency where the bottom teams can beat the top teams. It's the same year in, year out.

I kept myself entertained today by fixing a chest of drawers for Gemma's parents. I woke up with some aches and pains again, but Gemma is great, she never lets me feel sorry for myself, so chest of drawers it was! It always amazes me how many pieces come with it, but I never have any left over when I'm finished. Not like my dad who always has pieces left over! He always says that he doesn't need them all, but a few months later things generally fall off what he's made, or otherwise they totally collapse. Maybe he should take something from those experiences?

As I'm writing this I have noticed that my hands are stinging and really sore. The doctor did say that they might get a bit like this, although maybe the pain is due to my hard work today. We'll have to wait and see what happens . . . but my eyes are heavy so I'm off to bed.

11/12/08 – No Sleep

Had a bad night's sleep last night as my legs were playing up, so I went to training and chatted to Damian about what I could do. He decided to ring the hospital to find out the best tablets to take, but also what I'm allowed to take. He only managed to get the answering machine of the doctor who is in charge, so we went on our regular run, which relieved the pain in my legs. At the moment though I feel like Forrest Gump.

We ran for about half an hour, which was enough to get my legs going again after a few days off. As per normal, Damian and myself talked each other's ears off. I can talk, but so can Damian, so we always have a good laugh. The doctor got in touch when we got back and said that I can take paracetamol, and if I'm really struggling I can take Ibuprofen, but she was not overly keen on, as it would probably mess up my blood count, so I think it's best if I stay away from them. Next thing she gives Damian a telling off, saying 'you'd better not be pushing him too hard!' I found that funny as he's always pushing me . . . he really is my rock at the moment.

12/12/08 – Charity

I had heavy legs today – maybe it was to do with yesterday's run – so got stuck into the weights as I wasn't feeling up to another run with Damian. After that I went for a swim, and spent time in the jacuzzi and sauna with Fletch (Michael Fletcher), our fitness coach. It was nice to get a change of scenery.

After I finished training I had two meetings, one with the Torquay United Supporters' Trust, and the other with a group that does leukaemia research. Both were very interesting and we talked about doing a 'blood day', which I liked, as blood donations are a must in order to save lives. There are simply not enough people donating. The leukaemia research is something that I'd love to get involved in. I'm excited about it all and really want to do something to raise awareness.

When I was told about my condition it took a while to figure it all out. The first thing I asked myself was 'why me?' Well, things happen for a reason in life. Each person is given a different path, and this one is mine, to help save people's lives, to be a part of something special – my mum always said I was special.

On the home front Gemma and I are finding things a bit difficult at the moment. Amylia is playing up and it's hard work. She's like a night owl. She tries to sleep throughout the day and then is awake through the night. As any parent will tell you, disturbed sleep is like someone hitting you across the head with a wet fish. She wakes at 12, 2, 4, and 6. It's so hard for Gem and I really feel for her. She never moans and just says 'thank God for coffee'. I try to do my fair share to help but it's hard with me training, and then coming home and feeling tired. So we're both tired as Gemma is doing so much. Like every relationship it's never easy, but we'll get through it.

13/12/08 – Tablets

I finally gave in tonight and went to bed as normal, but I had a terrible night's sleep, as I couldn't keep my legs still and was in so much pain. I got myself out of bed and went downstairs at about 3.30 a.m. with the blanket from the spare bedroom. I got myself some paracetamol, which I was going to try to stay away from, but I couldn't take the pain anymore. After a while the tablets started to kick in, and I finally got to sleep at about 5.30 a.m. – relief!

I went to see the lads in action today against Bath City in the FA Trophy, and I froze my balls off! It was a boring game, not much of a crowd, but the result was good. Believe it or not but this was actually Torquay's lowest ever home attendance with just over 1,000 spectators turning up. At least we won 2–0 though, so who knows, maybe we'll be off to Wembley again?

I was looking forward to my night in with Amylia watching *X Factor*, as Gemma was out for a drink with her friends – something that she really deserves. Alexandra won, and it was great considering she didn't make the live shows a few years before that. It just goes to show where having a never-say-die attitude can bring you, and I hope to take something from that. After that I watched Klitschko v Rahman for the heavyweight title, and Klitschko is now expected fight David Haye. That will be a great fight, but I can't wait to see Haye get knocked out, because it still hurts after seeing him beat my mate Enzo.

14/12/08 – Fight Night

It would be nice to wake up just one morning and not have pain in my legs. I wonder how long it will take for it to stop. It is a common thing to get this type of pain, as it's one of the many side-effects that come from taking the tablets. It's the worst pain I have ever experienced, and the only way to describe it is for you to imagine getting into a bath that was roasting hot and you couldn't get out. They felt like they were going to explode, and the only thing that helped them was if I shook them around like crazy. I'm sure it looked rather odd to the people around me.

I managed to walk over to Gemma's parents' house with Amylia and had a bit of a heart-to-heart with them. They told me that they were worried about me, and advised me to speak to someone about my problems. If I'm being honest I think they're right – I'm struggling at the moment. The problem is though that I'm too stubborn.

When I describe myself as stubborn I mean that I am very set in my ways. If I get something in my head it is very hard to convince me otherwise, as I am very strong-willed. I'm not saying that I won't listen or change my mind, but you just have to show me you're worthy of your argument. This can sometimes take up to an hour for me to come around, as my missus will tell you.

Stubbornness of course can have positive attributes too. If someone tried to tell me that I couldn't achieve at something I won't listen. It would just make me try that little bit extra to succeed. For example, when I was in Penlan Comprehensive School there was one particular teacher, a gymnast coach. I think he found me to be pig-headed and a bit one-track-minded, as I always told him that I was going to be a footballer. He used to laugh at me and say, 'You've got no chance of ever being a professional football player'. To say his comments hurt me would be an understatement. It used to anger me, but at the same time it made me more determined to prove him wrong.*

* 2011 – *The only ones who this does not apply to are my two little girls who have this special hold over me, almost like magic. Whenever I tell them off, or get angry with them for not doing what they are told they just give me this big smile. Their smiles make me crumble every time. Gemma says that I'm a soft touch and that the girls have me around their little fingers. For once I can't argue with that and will just have to agree.*

Tonight was James' first professional fight and it was an amazing feeling. When he came out and stepped into the ring I really was the proudest brother in the world. He worked so hard for tonight and I really can't imagine what was going through his mind. I remembered my own professional debut against Northampton and it was incredible – but I had a team around me. He was there, on his own, one-on-one. But he loves what he does. When James came down to the ring he had my jersey on, with my name and number, which was a really nice touch and I got very emotional over it. I love him so much and he will always be my little brother. My prediction was a second-round knockout for James, but unfortunately it didn't pan out in the way any of us had hoped for.

It was some fight though: four three-minute rounds. I would have given the first round to James' opponent, the second and third to James and the fourth round was an embarrassment as James boxed the ears off him. To be fair I thought it was going to be an easy decision for the ref . . . but in my opinion he bottled it. The other fella was a good fighter in fairness to him, but the end result was a draw, which wasn't deserved, and the whole crowd knew it. The promoter though did say that he expected both of the lads to be fighting for British titles in the very near future. James was gutted though, but I know for sure, with time, he will have a good future in the world of professional boxing.

15/12/08 – Boxing

Last night was so emotional. My parents must feel that they are on a rollercoaster considering what's going on with us all. I got up and felt like I had just lost a cup final, and I wasn't even boxing last night. I was still hurting for James. He wanted it so bad. He is a Todd after all – a winner. I spoke to him earlier and he is still gutted by the result. He has tried to sort out a rematch for a couple of months down the line, but I don't think it will happen – especially if the other lad has any sense.

I was in the hospital with all my mates. That's what I call the staff and patients there now. They all know me by name and it makes me feel like I'm a part of their little family. These people are amazing. I got some results a little earlier and they were excellent. Dr Caroline said, 'Chris, great news. Your count has come down to 43.' Basically it had dropped 100. My 'count' is the number of white blood cells floating around in my blood. A normal level is between 3 and 8 (thousand million per litre of blood). I had far too many white blood cells and these were 'leukaemic' cells. As the imatinib kicked in, the number of leukaemia cells came down (good!) and left me fairly soon with just a normal level of normal white blood cells (non-cancerous/leukaemic ones). When I found out my blood count I just couldn't believe it – what a feeling! I had such a big smile on my face and looked like a Cheshire cat. It made everyone so happy when I told them, and gave me such a lift to see the smiles on my family's faces.

To top that all off I got a call from my other brother, Thomas, who said, 'I have some good news for you.' He had been trying to sort out the charity match, which I mentioned earlier, which would feature a Chris Todd XI versus a Joe Calzaghe XI at the Liberty Stadium, and it looks as though it's going to happen. I'm so lucky to have a family like mine. On the health side of things my legs are better tonight, and after so much good news in the one day, it's like all my Christmases have come at once.

16/12/08 - Thanks Lucy

The pain in my legs is starting to ease off which is brilliant. I have been on such a high after yesterday and had no training today as the lads are resting for Saturday's big game against Histon; it's a must-win game for us. I brought Amylia to the park today and she went on a swing for the very first time. I'm not sure if she liked it though, couldn't quite judge, but I wasn't pushing too hard . . . really.

I finally made a call earlier that I've been meaning to do for a while now. It was to someone who I will remember for the rest of my life, quite frankly because she could very well have been the girl who saved it. Her name is Lucy Grainger, and she was the nurse at the hospital who thought something was wrong with my blood. It's amazing really as doctors are always getting the credit, but it was a young nurse who noticed there was something wrong. How do you thank someone for that? You can't really. But I still did it. I thanked her from the bottom of my heart, and I think my phone call meant as much to her as it did to me. She said it was nice to have some good news. It's not every day that someone rings you and says, 'You probably saved my life'. Thanks again Lucy.

17/12/08 - Strange Day

Today was a funny day. On my way to training I saw my postman who was cycling down the road on his bike as normal. It was a bit frosty so you can imagine what happened next. He went arse over tit! At first I thought it was funny, but suddenly I thought he could have seriously hurt himself. He was sprawled across the road, yet I still didn't know whether to laugh or cry. So I drove over to him and said, 'Are you OK, mate?' to which he simply replied 'Bloody ice.'

He got up, brushed himself down, and just got on with it. God bless the Royal Mail. That wasn't the finish of it though. I drove on for a minute, and as I was going around the corner some crackpot coming from my left-hand side decided to come around too, and well let's just say it was a near miss. We both skidded to a stop but for a minute I thought we were going to have a serious accident. Luckily I was still in a fit of giggles over the incident with the postman, or I would have lost it. He did say sorry. What a journey to training though!

After training Amylia and myself went to Swansea on the train to the see the family, and I have got a meeting at Liberty Stadium tomorrow about the charity match. I've arranged to go out with my brothers later for a few drinks given that I have the chance, and it's something we haven't done in a while. I picked my brother Liam up, and if my day hadn't been funny enough, we were stuck behind a learner driver who smashed so many wing mirrors off parked cars I lost count. We've all been there. You would have thought she was drinking though, and when we overtook her, the driving instructor was pulling in her own wing mirror which was hanging off. She was smiling away as if nothing had happened – haha!

18/12/08 – Disappointed

Last night was amazing. It was great to be out again with my brother and I don't think we left the dance floor all night. My legs were killing me, but with a few drinks inside me it didn't really bother me – and yes, I can have a few just as long as I don't go silly. It is Christmas after all.

The meeting at the Liberty Stadium today didn't go well. When I arrived it was nice to see some of the old Swansea lads. The meeting didn't start at all well as Enzo completely forgot about it and we couldn't get hold of him. No surprise really, he is a boxer after all, although if he reads this he'll probably give me a swift jab and knock me out. I suppose all sports people are the same – it's not as if I don't forget anything. . . . The people we were there to meet were not happy with the fact that we had used the stadium's name already as the host ground, especially considering nothing had been signed. They said that as a result if the match didn't go ahead it would look bad on them. Then came the bombshell! If it did go ahead it would cost between £10,000 and £15,000 to stage. I couldn't believe what I was hearing. To take that much away from what we were trying to achieve would have been shocking. As you can imagine, I left the meeting extremely disappointed. I don't know what to do now. I guess we simply can't hold it there.

19/12/08 – More Shopping

I went into town do some Christmas shopping with my dad and brothers. It's not often we're all together so it was nice to spend the day together. Town wasn't too busy – I guess it's the credit crunch. I saw a lot of old friends and they were all showing their support for me. It's a nice feeling and makes me feel proud to think that so many people care. All those years of being a good friend and a nice person seem to have paid off! I always told myself, treat people how you want to be treated yourself.

When we got back to sunny Devon we were locked out, as Gemma was at her Christmas party. We couldn't get hold of her for a while, so were stuck in the car until we managed to get in touch, and she drove back. It's lucky that she wasn't drinking. We were in the car for an hour; dad, mum, Amylia, and myself, and played a quiz that my dad won comfortably – he's such a boffin. But, to be fair, he didn't have much competition.

On the health front I keep getting pains in my legs, but it's bearable. I just have to keep moving.

20/12/08 – Great Result

I went into town with mum and dad before today's game against Histon to do a little shopping. Well, my mum went shopping . . . we went to the footie. The team played really well and comfortably won 4–1. It was a great result, and I'm really starting to miss being on that field. Today's game would have been just up my alley, as Histon are a direct, strong, physical side. It's not long now until the big man's back on that field. After the game I checked on the other results, and they all won: Burton, Cambridge and Kidderminster. After the game I went to the Trust kids' Christmas party. The kids loved it, and I played pass the parcel, something which I hadn't done in years. I felt like a big kid, looking forward to Christmas, and just happy to be alive.

I just remembered an old interview I heard where the great rugby player Jonny Wilkinson said something that made a lot of sense. The question was, 'Jonny, how would you feel if you were told you could never play again?' He replied, 'When I draw a picture of myself I draw a picture of me smiling, holding the World Cup in one hand, and a rugby ball in the other, with my wife and kids standing next to me. But, if you were to take away the World Cup and the rugby ball what would you see? The answer is me, standing there with my family, and still smiling.' He said that after health and happiness comes everything else.

21/12/08 – What a Price!

I didn't have a great deal of sleep last night – partly my own fault, but also my legs were playing up. I went to meet a few of the lads and their partners for a Christmas drink that turned into a right session for the girls – not for me though as I was the designated driver, and the lads have a game coming up. The missus had a few, bless her, and I think we got in at 4.00 a.m. At one stage I had to go to a kebab shop to get some food, as I needed to eat in order to take my tablet. It's not something I would usually do when I'm not drunk. I went back into the pub, and before I took my tablet I showed it to all the lads, as they wanted to know what it looked like. They were amazed when I told them that just one tablet costs £22.

22/12/08 – Good News

I had another bad night's sleep, up and down all night due to my legs, and it's really beginning to get me down. This morning though I did a bit more Christmas shopping, went to get my blood done, and later on I returned for the results. Well let's just say that I received the best possible news from the doctor, as he told me that my blood count is down to 10.3. I'm only going to have to keep taking the Glivec once a day, and don't require any further treatment. I have to get a spleen test done soon to see if that has decreased, and if so I will be back on the pitch sooner than I had originally thought. Also, to help me with the pain in my legs I can start taking paracetamol on a regular basis. I couldn't wait to tell my family today . . . what a great early Christmas present!

23/12/08 – Christmas Presents

I went out and got my hair cut as I was beginning to look a little rough around the edges. My hairdresser Vanessa is sometimes a bit freaky as she is a bit of a mind-reader – she can work out so easily what I want. But now I'm back to my handsome self, thanks to her!

After a bit of last-minute shopping I drove down to my second home, Torbay Hospital, to give out some Christmas presents with some of the other players. It's so easy to do, but actually means so much to the kids. They love it and even think that we are really famous! On a serious note I believe that it's something that all clubs should do more of. It's only a half hour out of your day, and to see how ill some of these kids are makes you think how lucky you are.

24/12/08 – Noddy Car

I know I'm starting to sound like a parrot, but I had a really bad night, and couldn't sleep. I was up at 5.00 a.m., made myself a hot water bottle, and took some paracetamol to try to ease the pain. But it didn't work, and I was tossing and turning until I gave up and had a bath an hour later. After that I managed to get a few hours' sleep in.

Gemma told me she needed the car, and as my brother came down yesterday from Swansea I was told to take my dad's car out. Well let's just say it's like Noddy's car, with Christmas lights all over it. When we were on the motorway the clutch started to go, and I thought I'd be stuck there. My street cred was damaged, but if I had broken down in this car it would have been ruined, and the lads would have hammered me.

I found training really hard today. I did a 12-minute run, and it hit me hard as the lungs were in full swing. By the end of it I was blowing out a lot, but felt great as it really opened my lungs up to a degree that I hadn't been doing over the previous few weeks. After the run we did some ball work, and I worked on my touch. I wouldn't say it's back to its best yet but I'm getting there. Then again, my dad and brothers have always said I never had one to start with!

It's Christmas Eve and I'm ready for tomorrow. It's amazing that every person spends so much money just for one day, and if all those people just gave £1 away, it would make such a difference in so many people's lives.

25/12/08 – Happy Christmas

A great day but it's come and gone so quickly, and all the money's spent! It's been nice to have the family down, but I'm sure it wasn't much fun for Gemma as she had to cook Christmas dinner for twelve. She really is a little 'gem'. I would like to say that I helped, but I'm no Gordon Ramsay. I've been so spoilt, it's just silly, but I do love it, and won't complain. The little one had her first Christmas and I think she loved it – not the presents though, just the wrapping paper. And yes, I was like Bob the Builder, putting toy after toy together. Tonight we played a few games and sang a few songs on the karaoke. I think the rub-down the other day really worked, as I haven't had much pain in my legs today.

26/12/08 – Festive Fixture

Amylia found it really hard to sleep last night as she was so wound up after such a busy day, so I didn't get the best night's sleep myself. The house was full of presents and family, and to top it all off I was up really desperate need of a bath as my left leg was in real pain, but at least it was just the one today.

Went to today's game against Weymouth where we won 1–0 with a solid team performance, starring Scott Bevan, who is beginning to look unbeatable in goal. A freezing wind blew through all day. The stand we sat in had no cover and before the game I had a run on the pitch; it all added up to a tired and cold Welshman by the end of it.

I returned home and the family was still down so we had a game of Deal or No Deal on the Wii, where I lost in the final to my dad. He's always winning no matter what we play . . . I reckon he cheats.

27/12/08 – Massage Machine

I couldn't do that much training today as my legs weren't the best, so I went for a nice, easy jog, and then did some quick foot work, but I must say they weren't moving too quickly. Got home and had a relaxing night with the family. Everyone was so tired and the only noise was coming from my massage machine going crazy on my legs.

28/12/08 – Funny Old Game

We were at home against Kidderminster today where we played well enough and could easily enough have won by five goals. But football's a funny old game, and we lost

1–0, missing a penalty with the last kick of the game. It's left a nasty dent in our championship challenge. I did, however, get to meet someone who has the same illness as me. It was nice to get the chance to ask each other some questions, and have a chat about what we've both been going through. It was like a game of cards and we were playing 'Snap'. On the health front, it was a good day. No problems and I felt a lot better.

29/12/08 – Trek

I paid another visit to the hospital today for a few blood tests. I wasn't seeing the doctor today, just getting the bloods done, and it's a fair old trek just for that. Gave a quick 'hello' to my friends there, and wished them a happy new year. There was no training today as the lads are off for a few days, so I went straight home afterwards to spend time with the family.

30/12/08 – Night Running

Normally when you get the day off work you look forward to having a lie-in, and generally just having the opportunity to chill out. Not for me though. The missus had so many jobs for me to do, it's always the same, 'Do this, do that, get the drill out, fix this, fix that . . .' I love it really though, as I'm quite handy at the old DIY. My father-in-law calls me 'Todd the Builder'. After I had all my jobs done I fancied a run and as James was down, we decided to go out together, and boy did he need it – he'd put on 2st over Christmas following his fight. We finally escaped at 9.30 p.m. and it was freezing, but I like running at night when the ground's hard and the air is cold – it keeps your cockles warm.

31/12/08 – New Year's Eve

Got a little sleep last night but at least it's the last of the year. I had a two-hour drive home to Wales so I can be with my family for the New Year. It's great to get the chance to spend it with them, as I haven't been there on New Year's Eve since I was 17 because of the fact that I normally have a game to play the following day. But not this year . . . for obvious reasons. A New Year is around the corner, and it's a chance for me to make a resolution . . . I will play again.

1/1/09 – A New Year

Had a great celebratory night with the Welsh today, but was very tired driving home. I was thinking to myself 'what a year I've had, some right ups and downs'. I got engaged. Amylia was born. I bought a new house. I played at Wembley (where I was at fault for the goal that lost the game for us). Oh, and I got told I had CML! Wow, that's one mad year. But let's hope that 2009 is going to be full of just good things.

2/1/09 – Hoping to be Back

I seem to put more weight on my left leg, and that's the one in which I experience the most pain. I received some good news from the hospital today, saying I had an appointment on Monday for my spleen, and if all goes well I could be back in training very soon – fingers crossed. The craziest thing is that I can't eat any fatty foods for 24 hours, and I'm not to eat any food for 6 hours before the appointment. I'm guessing it's that the fat will show up around the spleen, but that's just a guess. I'm no scientist, that's for sure.

Swansea City days back in the old Third Division versus Kidderminster.

earning my trade across the water with Drogheda United. (Courtesy of Sportsfile)

Exeter v Morecambe, 2007. Here I am (below) with Adam Standfield (RIP), a friend who is truly missed.

My first away game after announcing my illness to the public and fans.

On the pitch at Woking showing the fans my appreciation for all their support.

Fighting back to fitness.

Matchday at Torquay. It's so good to be back on the pitch.

Support from the Torquay players – holding my jersey up in respect.

Me and Broughty on loan at Salisbury where we formed a great partnership.

Strike it lucky! At Wembley with Torquay United.

The icing on the cake after the final whistle at Wembley.

Utter relief and joy shared with Bucks.

Trophy celebration. Here I am with my biggest supporters – my mum and dad – at Wembley.

What a team!

With my winner's medal at Wembley – what an incredible feeling.

Victory parade.

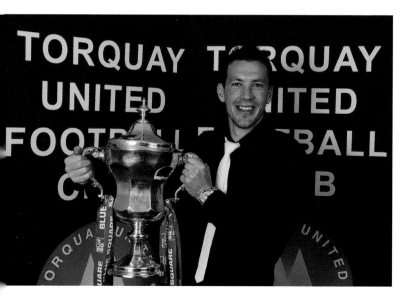

Torquay United, Blue Square play-off trophy delight.

The start of the rest of our lives: Gemma and I on our wedding day.

The Torquay squad at our wedding reception.

In the blood, fighting for a good cause.

Brothers in arms at Charity Fight Night. Left to right: Me, Liam, Gemma, James and Thomas.

Amylia and I share a moment of joy after a Newport County match.

Goal celebration for Newport.

Here I am with the Blue Square South winners' trophy for Newport County. Below: My super wife Gemma deserves a trophy.

Gemma and I with Welsh legend Mark Hughes.

With my kit for my new team, Forest Green Rovers.

The gaffer shows off his new talent. Jamie Turley, Rovers boss David Hockaday and me.

...mylia's Christening. From left : Steve (dad), Julie (mum), Gemma, Lyn (Gem's ...um) and Brian (Gem's dad).

...oddy's Angels.

Me and my nanna and bamba Fussell.

Me and my bamba Todd.

Publicising the first edition of More Than Football in the Blood. *Above: With Martin Worth, Jordan Smith and (bottom right) friend Ben Wedgery.*

Right: With Helen Chamberlain and Rocket from Soccer AM.

3/1/09 – Cup Success

Had a rough night, so feeling like shit. I think Santa has left his sack under my eyes. It's my own fault though as I forgot to take my tablet before I went to bed. That's the first time it's happened since starting the treatment. Well, let's just say my body sure let me know – I was up at 2.30 a.m. as I was in a really bad sweat. I think it's your body's way of saying 'you silly fool, get out of bed and take your pill'. So as soon as I realised I had forgotten, I went downstairs and took my 'Super Pill'.

Today has been good, as I went to watch the FA Cup game against Blackpool who we beat 1–0 (or should I say hammered them 1–0). What a result and I'm so pleased for the lads. I just wish I was out there with them. Maybe I'll be back for the next round, and I'm still hoping for Swansea or Arsenal away. Maybe it's written in the stars to draw one of my own teams. One thing I do know for sure is that I'm starting to feel good about myself.

4/1/09 – Cup Draw

Bucks gave me a ring last night and asked me to come along to watch the draw for the FA Cup with all the lads. He's been really good to me, and has involved me in everything that's taken place. He really is a first-class manager, and a really good friend.

I first met Bucks back in 2005 when he was brought into Exeter as player/coach by Alex Inglethorpe. I soon began to notice that he was a very gutsy person, which was something I liked about him – he was a real winner. I don't think there was a game where the two of us didn't come to blows. This was because we were both winners and always wanted the best outcome from games.

I really felt a great respect for him. A year or so later Inglethorpe parted company with the club and went to the Spurs youth team. Paul Tisdale was brought in and it was the start of a new era with Bucks made player/assistant-manager. This partnership worked well, with Bucks being the enforcer and 'Tis' the cool, calm thinker. With this combination they soon formed a squad worthy of success and in 2006 we reached the play-off finals only to fall at the last hurdle, losing 2–1 to Morecambe. To this day I believe if Bucks had played in that Wembley final we would have won.

After the summer break Bucks got his break as manager, at rivals Torquay United. A few days later I received a call from our Director of Football, Steve Perryman, to say that the club had received a bid for me from Torquay. In the end the decision was made simple for me. I asked Exeter if I could have an extension to my contract as I only had a year left on it and obviously wanted more security. This was refused, so once I was told that they could not commit to anything I knew where my destiny lay. It was a wrench leaving though, as I loved the club and was the club captain. Bucks offered me a three-year deal on a bit more money, and I always thought that he would make a good manager so I took the chance. I knew that the Exeter fans then couldn't understand why I left for their rivals just down the road, but I had to look after my livelihood and my family. The decision to leave was the right decision and achieving success with Bucks in 2009 was the icing on the cake.

Anyway, back to the match – it was an exciting build-up. Everyone was talking about who we were going to draw, how many tickets each of us would need, etc. Then the draw began, and what a disappointment it was when all the big boys came out, and we were still in the hat. By this point all you could hope for was a home tie. We were drawn out eventually, and got a home tie against Coventry City. It wasn't a bad draw really, and the fact we were at home gave us an even better chance to beat them. Still gutted though that we didn't get a bigger team.

5/1/09 – More Results

Had my spleen (and blood) checked today and it's dropped to 12.5cm. I will not find out until later if it has reduced enough to allow me to play again. I went to training straight after. Damian, Fletch and all the injured players went for a run that started off at a nice pace, before Damian decided to speed it up a little. It was some run, what a pace, but it felt great, and I was loving it. Just to be able to open up is an amazing feeling, considering the previous few weeks. At the end of the run Fletch jokingly said to me 'you're not ill!' It was great to hear that from somebody else. After training I went back to the hospital to discover my fate. There was a long wait to see the doctor, which prolonged the agony. I just wanted to play again. When I finally got into him he said, 'I have good news for you. Your blood count is good, and your spleen is at a normal size for someone of your size.' This was unbelievable news, music to my ears, and I couldn't stop smiling. I'm back. It's felt like I haven't played in a lifetime (even though it's only been a few months). There have been times when I thought that I wouldn't play again, but I just kept telling myself, 'don't worry, I'll be back'. I can't wait to kick on from here and get back on the pitch. One thing I will say for sure, I will never again take things for granted.

6/1/09 – Stressed Out

After a good night's sleep I got up, and my legs were feeling fine. I just hope it lasts. Having received the good news the day before I was looking forward to tonight's game against Burton, but I got a call off Northy to say the game was off – gutted. But at least I will be back when the game is finally played.

Today I just chilled out and got up to date with my odd-jobs. We've been sorting out the wedding arrangements and wow, do I feel sorry for the missus. She's so stressed out and I don't help (I am a man after all). Honestly, I do try, but then am just told I get in the way, so I leave her to it.

7/1/09 – David Beckham

Had a great day today, just me and my little princess (Gemma has been out and about, sorting stuff for the wedding). All we do is play with her toys and sleep – she is just like her dad – loves a cuddle. I went for a run in the freezing cold again today; it's really bitter out there, but I can't help myself and I'm really looking forward to training tomorrow.

I write a blog on the BBC sports website every week – well, actually I don't write it, I just tell my story to an exceptional writer named Brent Planck. He's really helped the blog to take off. A week or so after I came out in the press (with the illness, obviously) I was offered the blog, and I saw it as a wonderful opportunity to show people the ins and outs of what I was going through, with the hope that it would make people more aware than ever that this can happen to anyone, even a professional footballer like myself. It works quite simply. Brent rings me every Friday, interviews me, and then rings back 30 minutes later with the final piece.

When I started I thought a few people would look in on the blog on the odd occasion, but to my amazement it became a real hit. Brent rang me and said that the webpage was receiving thousands of hits from all over. I started to receive letters and gifts on a daily basis, which became overwhelming. Today's blog was on the main football page, and the link (with my picture) was next to the one and only David Beckham. I was well chuffed . . . two good-looking lads there.

8/1/09 – Back in the Mix

I went into training today thinking that I was just going to be doing some more intense stuff with Damo. The gaffer saw us jogging and asked if I wanted to join in. With zero hesitation I shouted over 'YES!' So I was back in the mix with a bit of keep-ball, followed by a small-sided game, and as I was feeling so well I decided to join in. It was an amazing feeling being back with the lads. After we finished I knew I was in for some extra work as Damo was setting up cones everywhere on the next pitch. I was blowing out of my arse, but it was so good to feel like that again. By the time we had finished I think I was waving a little white flag. I was done, and was feeling it to. I went in for a little massage from Tammy that just felt like heaven on my skinny legs. I got home to find my two girls sleeping on the sofa, and as my missus had to go to work I took over, the little one and me. I must say, it was well needed.

9/1/09 - Aches and Pains

I had a few aches and pains today, but overall I had a good day and I'm feeling good. I joined in with the main training again, and especially enjoyed the corner work as I was back doing what I do best, and that's banging in the goals with my nut. I really do fancy myself whenever we get a corner, as it's one of my main strengths. I really can't wait for my first game back, and to be honest if Bucks said to me tomorrow 'I want you to play', I'd snap his hand off. I have also rejoined the car school with the lads, so things are beginning to really get back to normal. Over the past few weeks I've been training at different times to the other lads, and the drive from Cullompton on my own has been a nightmare. The car school is made up of three of us, all travelling from Exeter. It had been four until Wayne started driving on his own – I'm sure that it's Martin Rice's fault he pulled out. It's now myself, Greavsey and Ricey, and the banter really flows between us. Ricey is a bit stale, always talking about dogs and cars . . . but I suppose it takes all sorts to make the world go around!

10/1/09 - Rugby Scrum

We beat Rushden & Diamonds in the FA Trophy this afternoon, winning 1–0 in a scrappy affair. Even the goal was like a rugby scrum, where we drove the ball over the line. Greavsey forced it over, and it was so funny, as he blatantly pushed one of the Rushden players. It was just lucky that the ref didn't see it. We're now through to the quarter-finals, which means just three games away from Wembley. Can you imagine going there for a third year running?

It was Amylia and myself at home on our own tonight, as the missus is away on her hen party. They've gone to Swansea, and all I'll say is look out Swansea, the 'Cullompton massif' is on its way. I was about to put Amylia in the bath when I noticed that she had a bad rash with lots of spots and sores, so I thought I'd better ring a doctor. I was told to take her down to the hospital in Tiverton so they could take a look at her, but the doctor just said that she had a reaction to taking solids, as she had just started. It's been nearly four days since I have had any pain in my legs. I don't want to jinx it, but maybe I have gone through the worst. Things are looking up.

11/1/09 – Fish

I decided to take it easy. Went to get some coldwater fish for the Spongebob Squarepants fish tank though! We got a little black one, and a red and white one. I would say that Amylia really loves them, but she just stares at them really, and I think it's more Gemma and myself who love them, rather than Amylia. We are like big kids at times. I was going to go for a run today, but my legs are a bit tired, and with my calf muscle being sore, I thought I would just leave it ready for tomorrow's training.

12/1/09 – More Aware

As the first team was not in training I joined in with the young players for the sessions. I enjoyed it, and I think I would just enjoy a kick around in the street at the moment, just to cherish every time I play. My leg held up well today, so let's hope it's nothing more serious than a bit of stiffness, because it's the same leg that I had the problem with before. When I got home we had to take the little one to the doctors as her back was still a bit sore, but it was good news as he said it looks just like dry skin.

I had a few phone calls today about doing some interviews for the BBC and Setanta. I'm really getting a lot of press since my diagnosis, which is great, as it makes people more aware. Since my diagnosis I have kept a diary. The day after I was given the news that I had leukaemia I thought that it would be good to write all my thoughts down, silly really – I mean, how could I ever forget? Then again . . . I am a very forgetful person. Somewhere down the line I'd hope to turn the diary into a book.

When I started writing I found myself in another world, a world that was for myself, somewhere where I could let my feelings out without hurting anyone else. Maybe I just hid behind the words, and found myself letting everything out of my mind. From the very first day I never wanted anyone to feel sorry for me as I have always believed that you have to believe you're well, and the last thing I needed was people making me feel worse by over-caring . . . although is that even possible?

I wanted people to treat me like they always had; the funny, friendly, little-bit-silly Chris Todd. As the days went by I started writing a day-to-day diary, something I never thought that I would do as, growing up, I always thought they were for girls to keep secrets in. If I'm totally honest, a diary written by me growing up, and taking into account the fact that I have dyslexia, would have been such a mess that I don't even think the CIA would have been able to understand it. I'm really glad that I have written so much down, as I believe that it has given me hope. I find myself looking forward to waking up, and seeing what's in store for me, then writing it all down as the day has gone on. It has given me a path, a real direction, and I started to see progress in myself.

13/1/09 – Getting Stronger

I had another good day's training, and am getting my strength back with each passing session. I am really starting to feel like my old self on the training pitch, and it was nice to put in a few tackles today, and have a bit of a tussle with the strikers, as I really do like that part of the game. After training I did some boxing with big Scott Bevan. That guy really packs a punch, but I guess that's what you'd expect from a 6ft 4in, 16-stone lad. He is the perfect sportsman, and knowing my boxing like I do, he would make a good pro-boxer. I spoke to Bucks today about getting some games, and he thinks it would be good for me to go out on loan, something that I have never done before, but it would be an experience. I can understand that I need games, and there are no reserve fixtures in this league, which is a disappointment, so a loan deal may be the right thing for me to do.

14/1/09 – Celebrity

I felt like a right celebrity today. It was meant to be my first proper day's training today, and it seemed that every Tom, Dick and Harry was there, from television stations and newspapers. I got some right stick from the lads who were saying it was 'The Chris Todd Show', and they were not wrong. I loved it, as I had always enjoyed giving interviews. My old centre-half partner Woodsy said, 'It's like a spaceship has landed around here today.' They filmed training and did interviews when it was finished. Setanta came back to my house for some more coverage, this time with the family. Gemma was so nervous, yet she still did brilliantly, but the star of the show was the little one – until she fell asleep. I think dad was boring her, to be honest. The coverage that I have received through my journey so far is astonishing. I'm even on Setanta for the live game against Wrexham on Friday night. It's a top-of-the-table clash, a real must-win for us, as Wrexham are beginning to look a serious threat.

15/1/09 – Reality

There wasn't so much press work today so it was back to reality, head down, working hard in training. I felt that I had put in a really good session which was encouraging, and at the end of it the gaffer had obviously recognised this as he pulled me aside and said, 'you're getting back to your best,' which was nice to hear. On the whole my days are getting back to normal. I am so tired when I get home, so at the minute I am topping myself up with protein and vitamins. That will help me in the long run I hope.

Oh yeah, I forgot to say earlier that one of the fish died. I couldn't believe it. Poor little fish. Dead after a few days. I'm just glad that the little one is too young to notice. But at least the black one is still alive. Maybe we should call him Darth Vader?

16/1/09 – Tricky Questions

My 'career' as a football pundit (although I think the correct terms is a 'match analyst') began tonight on Setanta and what an experience it was. It was so much fun, and I didn't make any mess-ups. That was a nice feeling. I was really conscious of trying not to say the wrong thing, and really had to think carefully before answering any of the tricky questions about the lads! I was told afterwards that if things didn't work out with the football that there was a job there for me – I don't know if they were serious or not – haha! Earlier that evening I did the 'chip challenge' on the pitch. For every one I got in they said they would give me £100 towards my charity. I excelled, as I managed to get 7 in. The lads couldn't believe it, and if I'm being honest, neither could I. A few of them watched on and gave me some stick. Lee Mansell was even wearing my Welsh boxer shorts. I was in my zone though and they didn't manage to put me off!

17/1/09 – Stag Party

I had the first part of my stag tonight, so got up early this morning to get ready for the big weekend ahead. I was worried, yet looking forward to it at the same time. Twenty-five in all decided to go, and from when I got up I knew it was going to be a rough weekend. We managed to get up there in one piece . . . well except for the Welsh gang. My dad was driving and a bird flew straight into the windscreen. When I saw the picture one of the lads sent me you would have sworn that a dinosaur had hit it. My dad was undeterred though (even after being told that the breakdown service couldn't get to them until the morning, and that everyone should sleep on the minibus) and drove on even with the smashed window. How he did this I really don't know. We had a great night and I'm fairly certain that we drank Nottingham out of beer. My cousin Carl's the worst – he's like a fish, and the lads from Devon couldn't get over him. They said he was like

Uncle Bryn from *Gavin & Stacey*. And before anyone asks I did remember to take my tablet with me, although I had to take it with a pint of Guinness and a packet of crisps, which I'm sure my doctor will love to know!

18/1/10 – Fancy Dress

I woke up this morning and needless to say I was feeling the worse for wear. It feels like I have a mouth full of sand, but it was a good night. Worth it? Definitely. There was no time to get over it as we were all going down to the pub for breakfast, and no, I couldn't handle a pint like some (Uncle Bryn). I stuck to bacon and eggs, washed down with a pint of Coke. After that I went back to the hotel to get changed, not into normal clothes but fancy dress. Let's just say I got the worst one, as I was dressed in all pink, like a fairy. What a mess I looked! If only the gaffer could have seen me. Once dressed we went for a game of indoor bowling. Imagine the scene – it was Bugs Bunny bowling against a wrestler on a Sunday afternoon in Nottingham. That night the lads had planned to go to a strip joint, but were gutted when they found out that it was closed. So what do you do when something like that happens? If you can't go to the stripper, the stripper can come to you. It was funny for the lads but not for me. She beat the hell out of me, hitting me across the chest, face and arse, with the lads shouting 'hit him harder!' I always thought a stripper was meant to be nice and sexy, not a happy slapper!

19/1/09 – Returning Home

We were all wrecked coming back from Nottingham, and I was so glad that I didn't have to drive. That was left to poor old Matt, my mate from Cully. I chatted for about 30 minutes, and then I was outers, and slept for the rest of the journey. When I got home I spoke to Gemma, and played with Amylia for a while, but was in bed from 2.00 p.m. until 7.00 p.m. I got up for some food, but then went straight back to bed. That's about the best you were getting from me today . . . well it was my stag weekend after all!

20/1/09 – TV Star

I did some more television work for BBC Wales today, as they came with me to the hospital when I was having my blood test. They are putting some footage together to make a video about my illness and recovery. I went to training after the test, and then they shot more footage of me at home. Gemma is really getting more comfortable in front of the camera, and I'm so proud of her.

I was gutted today as tomorrow's game has been called off. It was meant to be my comeback game against my local team Cullompton. It would have been good to have had a run out but maybe it's better to rest my leg until it's right. What's the saying? Don't run before you can walk?

21/1/09 – Wedding Dress

Gemma and I were originally planning on getting married in June, but decided to bring it forward to February after my diagnosis. We also decided to have a bigger wedding than we had previously planned. The decision to bring the wedding forward was a joint one. We sat down and were honest about the whole situation. Were we rushed into it? Yes, but for the right reasons. We planned to get married within the next year or so anyway. We were both scared, and really didn't know how mine, or Gem's dad's health was going to pan out.

However, today could have been a massive upset in terms of the wedding. Gemma and my mum were talking about different stuff to do with the wedding, and mentioned the dress. Gemma had picked out the dress in October, and was told that she would be contacted when it was ready. She phoned them last Friday and Saturday, and emailed them on Sunday but never got any reply. She finally managed to contact the seamstress who gave her the disturbing news that there had been a fire, gutting a restaurant and fishmongers beside the bridal shop, which had extensive smoke damage. We were both distraught. Now what were we to do with no dress and less than two weeks before the wedding?

It was all kicking off, with Gemma going mad at this lady, as she was no help in getting hold of the shop's owner. Then the lady threw her a lifeline, saying that she had five dresses at home that she was fixing, but hadn't a clue if any of them was Gemma's as there were no names on them. Gemma decided to drive to the woman's house to find out if one of them was hers, and thank God it was. Gemma was chuffed, and so was I . . . it could have cost me more money!

Had more camerawork with Sky today, as they were at the house to interview us, and let's just say that the missus is really taking to this. She was actually talking over me. Funny what a bit of confidence can do for someone.

22/1/09 – A Chance

I did some more press work after training, as it's FA Cup week this week, so everyone is wanting a bit of press with the club, and yes, they all want a bit of the Todd – haha! The lads must be getting fed up of me as I'm on everything! Before training the gaffer pulled me aside, and gave me some great news – I'm back in the mix for the FA Cup game this weekend. What a feeling and as a result I've been on such a high today!

On the health front I'm feeling really good. My doctor said that I'm still in good range with my blood, and should keep taking my 'super-tablet' once a day.

23/1/09 – Dummy

I woke up this morning and couldn't believe what I had done. Last night I forgot to take my tablet. I took it as soon as I remembered though – the doctor told me that if I ever forgot, I should take it as soon as I remember. What a dummy I am.

It's the day before the big FA Cup game and I hope to make the bench. You can have seven players on the bench for cup games, and it's something that I think the league should consider doing, as it would be a lot better for players and managers alike. With the game being tomorrow, the starting XI won't train for very long, but as per usual I did my extra bit with Northy, which is a help, and then I hit the gym. I did all I could today, and put in a good case for getting on the bench . . . it's all down to the gaffer now.

24/1/09 – Bench

Today was the first time in months that I have had to get my bag ready for a match. I was really buzzing – it's amazing thinking about what you take for granted. The ground was electric when I arrived. The one phrase I kept hearing was 'it's good to have you back'. I walked into the changing room and there it was, my jersey, hanging on my peg, with 'Todd 6', on the back. In my head I thought I was going to make the bench, but I didn't even make the squad. I knew it was a big ask, and realised that it was going to be hard to get my place back. Hopefully I won't have to wait too long though. We were playing Coventry City in the FA Cup in front of over 6,000 supporters, and all I can say is how on earth did we lose the match? It was 1–0, with Coventry scoring in the 87th minute. We dominated the match, but I suppose if you don't take your chances . . .

After the game I had the opportunity to talk to the Coventry manager Chris Coleman. We had first met six or seven years ago and he remembered me – we are both Swansea lads. Turns out we had the same youth team manager, Ron Walton, in our days at Swansea City. He went through a pretty tough time himself, as in January 2001 he broke his leg in a car crash, an injury which he never recovered from, and which ultimately led to the end of his playing career. It was good to speak to him, and look for advice from him about his recovery. He really is a top man, and I'm grateful that we had the chance to speak.

25/1/09 – Gunners

I managed to get hold of two tickets to watch Cardiff versus Arsenal in the FA Cup at Ninian Park. I brought my dad with me (we both support Arsenal – and Swansea of course), something we haven't done since I was about 15, so it was really nice. The only downside was that the ticket was in the Cardiff end. If Arsenal had scored we would have had to have stayed in our seats and kept quiet! It would not have gone down too well – two

Swansea lads jumping up and down in the Cardiff end! It was a poor game, ending 0–0, but it was good to see Arsenal up close.

They have some real athletes in their team . . . they didn't look bothered though. How can they think that way, when they are paid millions a year? Given half a chance I would play for free to pull on an Arsenal shirt.

Still trying to sort everything for the wedding. It's beginning to get on my nerves a bit. A part of me wishes we had done it as we originally planned, i.e. going away. Oh well, it will all come together in the end – I hope.

26/1/09 – Good News

I got a bombshell today as I found out that Lee Hodges was not travelling to tonight's game. Lee is the first-choice centre-half, and I thought to myself that I must be in with a shout. But no, I didn't get a sniff. Maybe the gaffer thinks I'm just not ready. That doesn't stop me being disappointed, and I'll just have to keep plugging away, and take my chance when it comes.

All that disappointment immediately vanished though as soon as I got home . . . Gemma's pregnant! I'm over the moon! Another little Todd on its way – wow! I must have some really good swimmers in me, and to think I had to go through all that effort at the sperm bank not too long ago – haha! I am a very happy man.

27/1/09 – Getting Excited

I trained with the youth team today, which was really enjoyable, but most importantly it was good for my fitness. The young lads are a good bunch, but it's a lot different to my own days as a youth team player. They don't get it half as tough today, and get away with murder. It's not down to the manager – it's just the way times have changed. I can still remember long afternoons cleaning at the Vetch Field, Swansea. I'll never forget the day I spent 4 hours cleaning the ground, only returning home from training for supper (not tea) at 8.00 p.m. After training at the Morfa Stadium, where the Liberty Stadium stands today, we would head back to the Vetch to clean up after the first-team squad. I can still picture the mess the rooms were in. They were really horrendous, with bottles and newspapers everywhere. It was our job to get it back to its best. On a normal day we would start at around 1.30 p.m. and be done within an hour.

That day we started off like every other day, like Snow White's seven dwarfs we all got stuck in. This didn't finish as an ordinary day though, because when we had finished our normal chores, Paul Morgan, our coach, came in to inspect the rooms. He always did this, making sure they were up to a proper standard before we could leave. Today, according to him, this wasn't the case. We were going nowhere. He wasn't happy and was picking us up for every speck of dust, and made us continue cleaning, over and over again. Two or three hours went by and you really could have eaten your dinner off the walls, never mind the floors.

He really was picking fault with anything and everything, saying something wasn't right. By this point the lads had enough and started kicking up a fuss, leading to a few of us speaking out of turn – me being one of the main instigators. Little did we know that it was a test of character that we had failed at the last hurdle, triggering Paul to punish us even more by making us get our kits back on for the running session from Hell, to the point of sickness. I really don't think the youngsters of today would have coped with just half of what we received.

After training I wasn't feeling well; my throat was sore and I had lost my voice. This wasn't good for me, as I love to talk. I rang the doctor who told me to come straight down for a check-up. I was down there all day, with no food or money. I was stuck with lots of free cups of tea and coffee while I waited. Good old NHS. It had killed Gemma's plans for today as we only have the one car at the moment to get around. She has lost a day to do things for the wedding, and was well stressed out as a result. I did, however, finally do something productive in relation to the wedding as I have managed to sort out a magician to keep the guests entertained. As the days are counting down, I'm really getting excited about our big day.

28/1/09 – Good Win

The lads won last night's game 2–0 away from home against Lewes. It's really hard to come away from places like that with 3 points. It's also hard when you're not playing. You're really chuffed for the lads, but if they are always winning, you'll never get a game. Trust me, every football player has been in this position and it really is a catch-22 situation. To make matters worse I felt really ill today. Even little Amylia is ill, bless her, which makes it harder on me. It was a lazy day. I don't think I got out of my pyjamas until after 2.00 p.m.

29/1/09 – Forgotten

I was feeling a bit better today after last night's events. I really think that it might have been that fruit I ate yesterday, as it played havoc with my stomach. It's amazing really that there's not a lot of tablets or medicine which you can safely take with this illness owing to the medication I'm already taking. This is to prevent them affecting any change in my blood.

It's hard enough being a pro-footballer in relation to being very limited in terms of what medicine or supplements you can take to bring you back to full strength when you get a cold or the 'flu, just in case you are giving yourself an edge to your game, even though all you're trying to do is get better. I think the FA should look into this for all players, as it really is a bit sketchy for my liking. By unknowingly taking the wrong supplement you could face a lengthy ban, and it's just not right.

Got the mop chopped today, ready for Sunday and it looks great thanks to my exceptional stylist.

I found out earlier that I'm not travelling to Southport with the squad, which I suppose isn't really a bad thing with the big weekend ahead. It does feel though that at the minute I am the forgotten man at the club. Head up though – big weekend ahead.

30/1/09 – Crazy Girls

I trained with the youth team again today to keep my fitness up but other than that I didn't have a lot planned . . . or so I thought. I got home to a house full of crazy girls, all Gemma's friends sorting things out and excited about the weekend. Being the gentleman that I am I offered to help out in any way I could. My job was to go to Tiverton, which is about a 15-minute drive away, to pick up the wedding cake. I went into the shop, requested the cake, and all I got in return was a shell-shocked face from the woman behind the counter. She said, 'There's a problem . . . we can't find the full cake, and we think somebody else has taken it by mistake.' Now, how do you tell a stressed bride that there's no cake with just two days to go? I have to admit that we were blessed that Marks and Spencers were so good to us. They tried their best to solve the problem, and came up with three tiers of cake, but two of the tiers were exactly the same. They were also giving us a free bottle of champagne and flowers. When I got home Gemma was happy . . . at least we had a cake, but she wasn't happy about the missing tier. She rang all the M&S stores in Devon to see if any of them had the missing tier, and found one, in of all places, Torquay. By this stage it was 7.00 p.m., and it was shutting at 8.00 p.m. So I had to get back in the car and travel there with time ticking away. It cost me £22 for the missing tier, and I was a happy man going home to my smiling, future wife.

I hope it's worth it . . . the cake I mean.

31/1/09 – Day Before the Big Day

It's the day before the big day and I'm ready. It's going to be one amazing day, something that I'm only doing once, and I can't wait. If you had said to me three years ago that I was going to be married I would have laughed at you. Then again, I never imagined I would be ill either. But I must say, Gemma is the one, my little rock, and I would be lost without her. I couldn't be happier. I love my family so much. Tonight we went out for a few quiet ones – that turned into a few more quiet ones, and eventually led to bed at 4.00 a.m. It really could have got out of hand, but I eventually called it a night, as I knew that I'd look a right mess in the morning with big black bags under my eyes. Can you believe it? Tomorrow I am going to be a married man.

1/2/09 – Wedding Day

I'm full of beans today, but a bit tired after last night's 'quiet ones'. I went down for some breakfast – that was well needed, as I needed to get ready for a lot more drinking. After that I went for a swing with the lads, and no, it's not the bedroom type – it was on the driving range! We played a game where you had to get your ball into a small-netted basket. Well let's just say that I won, and the lads were gutted. Afterwards we went back to the room to get ready. There was a lot of work to be done, but in the end I looked a right class sight . . . picture a good-looking Welshman in a white suit with a black tie. I loved the whole occasion, and wasn't nervous, but they started kicking in when the first guests started to arrive. OK, I was bricking it!

Having the wedding at home in Devon meant that we could invite as many people as we wanted, so that's what we did and decided to ask every man, woman, and dog we knew. To say it was a big wedding would be an understatement – there were 350 guests there. Funny as it sounds I'm sure there could have been a lot of wedding crashers there, as the next morning we both said that we didn't recognise a few faces. It truly was a day to remember for so many different reasons.

I waited, and waited, and then Gemma entered the room. She was like a princess, and I'm pretty sure she cried all the way down the aisle. How I didn't crack I don't know! When I put the ring on her finger there was never a better feeling. It was a great day and night . . . from what I can remember.

During my football career I have made a lot of good friends and many of them turned up on the day, so I will take this chance to say thanks to all the lads from Plymouth and Exeter – oh, and of course to the Torquay boys. The full Torquay squad were in attendance, as well as the management staff. From my Exeter City days we had Paul Tisdale, Julian Tagg (Chairman), Steve Flack, Billy Jones, Matthew Gill, Danny Seaborne and Paul Jones, as well as Jamie Mackie and Garry Sawyer. The lads were all well happy when I told them I was getting married. I think they just wanted to take their 'rascal' suits out and were thinking ahead to the after-party.

2011 – It truly was a day to remember for so many different reasons, and was a very emotional time for both Gemma and myself. We are glad we got married then, but we renewed our vows in summer 2011. The main reason for this is that we feel there was something missing, maybe it's because a couple of years ago we felt it was more a celebration that I was still there, or maybe we missed out on the whole church thing. Whatever it was, the fact is that we are in a happy place right now, with Gem's dad and I both being a lot healthier – and with the arrival of Alanya we feel like a complete family.

2/2/09 – Loan Ranger

Today's the first time I've woken up as a married man, and I couldn't be happier. I have the most perfect wife in the world. I woke up with the biggest smile on my face, and no, it's not for the reason that you may be thinking . . . although I suppose that had a big part to play (wink, wink). We got up, went downstairs and had our wedding breakfast. We cleaned the hotel out of it and then headed home to chill out. It's amazing how one day can take so much out of you.

Then the phone rang, it was the gaffer. He said, 'Do you want to go on loan to Salisbury to get some games? If you do then you'll have to come down to the ground pronto before the window closes.' No chance to catch up on some missed sleep them. So off I went in search of first-team football. I arrived home three hours later as a Salisbury player (for a month anyway). I am really looking forward to it. Salisbury is in Wiltshire and the club there a full-time outfit that are struggling at the bottom of the Conference. It's great that I'm going to be playing in the same league as Torquay, only this time at the other end of the table. I've been told that it's a friendly, family club, and I'm really looking forward to the games and the challenges that lie ahead.

Salisbury is completely different to both Torquay and Exeter. Torquay truly does live up to its name as the 'English Riviera', and has also drawn favourable comparisons with the French city of Montpellier. It developed into a beautiful seaside town resort in the nineteenth century (before that it had been a fishing and agricultural area) that holds so many hidden treasures. If it had the weather to match it then people wouldn't have to be paying those ridiculous air-traffic taxes to fly abroad. Some of the beaches are the best I have ever seen. I even proposed to Gemma overlooking Babbacombe Beach. It's a must for everyone visiting Devon.

Exeter is such a laid-back city (around 16 miles from Torquay) that offers a lot of culture to see, with one of the best cathedrals around which has a large astronomical clock. There honestly must be a coffee shop on every individual street corner. The city is expanding all the time, along with its football and rugby teams.

3/2/09 – Snowing

It was snowing again today, and Torquay's scheduled game against Weymouth was called off. It would have been a good chance to get 3 points, as the other teams weren't playing either. It was a great opportunity though to chill out, and catch up with some shut-eye after the weekend. In the afternoon I went outside to make Amylia's first ever snowman, something which I have not done since I was a little boy. While I was making it for her you would have sworn it was for me. It was great fun. Let's be honest, most fathers are really big kids.

We went out for our first meal since the wedding as Mr and Mrs Todd – great food, and so much to talk about.

4/2/09 – Practice Match

We had a practice match today, and it was great to get some minutes under my belt, to help with my match sharpness and fitness especially. After the game Bucks pulled me aside and said that he was very pleased with me lately. I knew I was performing well but I guess I have to remind other people how good I was in the past, and still am today, and that's what I will continue to do.

After training I went to Pro-Direct Sports, where I had been offered some boots by the owner a few months back; he told me to come back when I was playing again. Now he has lived up to his word, and I got two pairs of Mizunos – the only make of boots that I wear. Then I was off to the hospital for my check-ups, and all the results came back with good news. I was told I'm a little bit anaemic, but that it's nothing to worry about.

5/2/09 – New Team-Mates

I had my first day of training with my new team-mates today. It's always hard when you enter into a new environment, as you feel the onus on you to fit in straightaway. The lads are a great bunch though, and it's nice to sometimes have a change of scenery and to meet new people. They had started the season really well and hit top spot in the league in early September. However, they suffered a number of injuries to key players and the form stopped. Then in October the club was forced to cut costs as they had failed to raise a £200,000 target to keep the club financially secure and a number of their top players were sent out on loan.

To break the ice I wore a Welsh shirt as one of the lads, Michael Fowler, is Welsh and gets a lot of stick for it, so I thought that I would give him a bit of support. They loved it . . . or was it more like they hated it? I'm not sure. Whatever, it did the trick and broke the ice. We had a really hard session in the gym where we biked, and rowed – that was really tough.

Competition is what brings out the best in a footballer, whether that's fighting for a trophy or having competition from another player who plays in the same position as you. In general I thrive on competition. I will say that no matter what I do, I have to win. I really am the world's worst loser.

6/2/09 – Training Indoors

Another good day of training today but we were still confined indoors because of the snow. It's not all bad though because you can get a real sweat on. The only problem is that I'll have to wait a little longer for my debut in a Salisbury shirt. So we're stuck up here now with no game, and we're not able to travel home because all the roads are too bad. So what do you do when there is no football, no kids, and a day off the next day? A night out with the lads for a bit of team bonding I suppose!

7/2/09 - Salsa Dancing

I'm so tired today. It's all my own fault, but it was well worth it. I don't think I got too much sleep, as we were up extremely late salsa dancing, would you believe?! Michael Fowler is learning it in his spare time. Picture three lads doing salsa dancing in a living room in the early hours of the morning, having had a few too many (and I have two left feet). You would have loved to have been a fly on that wall. Thank God BBC Wales, Sky or Setanta were not there that day to film me!

We drove home to Devon in the afternoon, and even though I had a blast the night before, I was looking forward to seeing my two special girls. I really miss them, and when I'm away it's hard.

8/2/09 - Cleaning

Had a great night's sleep, and when I got up Gemma had plans for me. She asked me to clean under the stairs, and to be fair I think everybody has got one place that is a mess. Let's just say that it took me some time to clean it. In the afternoon Amylia and me were invited over to my mother-in-law's for some Sunday dinner. It was good to get some home cooking. After dinner I fell asleep, like you do when you have a full belly.

9/2/09 - Astroturf

I was back in training with Torquay today, and it was nice to see the lads again. We trained on the Astroturf as the training ground was waterlogged due to the melting snow. When we got on the pitch it still had a bit of snow on it, so the lads, being the big kids that they are, had a massive snowball fight against the youth team – which we won. It was such a buzz! For some reason all of that got me thinking about what it must be like for all our soldiers out in Iraq and Afghanistan. I have so much respect for the guys, and have a few mates in the marines. If I was not a footballer I think that's probably what I would be doing. It would sure be different from throwing a few snowballs – ducking and diving away from real bullets and fighting for your life is scary stuff. Good on you guys.

10/2/09 – Cup Game

I was waiting around today on a call to say whether tonight's game against Swindon Supermarine in the Wiltshire Cup was on or off. But as it had been snowing all week, then raining last night, my hopes weren't set too high. The call eventually came and it was game on! This will be my first game back since 23 September 2008. I feel reborn. What a feeling!

Salisbury were 3–2 down from the first leg, so a win by two goals was required. The competition may have been only the Wiltshire Premier Shield (a single-county cup competition involving clubs based in Wiltshire) but to me it was like I was playing in the European Cup. The game itself was a really good chance for me to get to know the way the lads played. There's only so much you can learn on the training ground. We won 3–1 in a hard-fought game, and I played the whole 90 minutes, something that hadn't been the original plan.

But I felt great and I think if the gaffer had tried to substitute me, he would have had to have literally dragged me off the pitch. I was back doing all the things I do best; heading, tackling, and I nearly ended up on the scoresheet. It was great to be back. It was so late when we were driving home that I asked James Bittner, who is in our car school, to pull over so I could take my tablet out of my bag in the boot . . . the things you gotta do just to keep yourself alive!

11/2/09 - Little Sore

I went to bed last night wondering how I was going to be feeling, but good news, I didn't feel too bad at all, just a little sore in the right leg.

Today Gemma and I became totally hitched as we opened a joint bank account. Is it a good thing? We'll just have to wait and see. Hopefully a few more shops will shut down because of the credit crunch before Gemma gets to them. It got me thinking back to Gemma's father's speech at the wedding. It went something like this, 'Sadly last week Chris lost his bankcard, but he's not that bothered and hasn't even reported it to the police. The reason? The person who found it has spent much less than what Gemma would have!'

12/2/09 - Growing Fast

I had to get Amylia a new car seat today, as she's outgrown her old one. She's growing so fast it's untrue. And to think, I used to laugh when my friends and family used to tell me when she was only a few months old that she would grow up so quick. How right were they? I haven't had the chance lately to spend a lot of time with my family as I have been travelling back and forth to Salisbury. In the afternoon I was on my travels again for training under the floodlights. It reminds me of my days in Ireland with

Drogheda United. As was the case with Drogheda at the time, Salisbury's squad is a mixture of full-time and part-time footballers, so the reason we trained at night was so the whole squad could train together. At least we trained on a pitch with floodlights. When I was with Drogheda we once trained in a field where the only light was the light coming from the streetlights – no exaggeration! It didn't matter much though as we won the next game.

13/2/09 – Debut

It's the day before my league debut for Salisbury, and I'll get my first taste of Conference football for quite some time. I went into training buzzing, and then came away annoyed as I'd got a kick on my foot and it went up like a balloon. I couldn't believe it, and all I was thinking about was whether or not I'd be able to play or not. After training I went into town to buy some Valentine's presents for Gemma. I made sure that I didn't spend too much money, as things are tight after the wedding. I returned to the digs with some nice bits and bobs. You wouldn't believe what we got up to though – we made Valentine's cards from scratch, and I mean scratch. They looked brilliant, as I am very artistic. You'd have paid good money for them in a card shop, and I even made one for Amylia. There's my soft side again. I iced the foot all night, and kept it elevated. It started to feel a lot better as the night progressed. Just hope it will be all good for tomorrow's game.

14/2/09 Hammering

Well the foot survived the night thank God, although it was still a bit black and blue, and I was ready for my return against one of the best teams in the league – what a start! I got to the ground and was really looking forward to it. Got ready for the warm-up, had a bit of treatment on my foot that did the trick. We did really well in the first-half, but went 1–0 down. We had most of the play though, lots of chances, but just couldn't put the ball into the net. The second half was what can only be described as a football nightmare. We got whipped. When we lost a goal to a doubtful penalty to go 2–0 down, the lads' heads dropped like I haven't seen in a long time. I guess that's what happens when you're down at the bottom of the table. The game ended up 4–0. It's never a nice feeling to lose by such a heavy scoreline. Personally I'm not used to losing by that margin.

After the game the gaffer kept us on the pitch for a while. He said some nice stuff about me, but for the other lads I'm sure they didn't enjoy what he said. He told me how well I had done, and it was great to see the commitment that I showed especially considering how long I'd been out for. Credit for playing football again? What a great feeling . . . but inside I was hurting about the result. Afterwards I drove back to Devon with Gemma and Amylia, as they had come to watch the game as a surprise. It was a really lovely touch, so we decided to stop off and have a meal for Valentine's Day. Just my two girls and me.

15/2/09 – Hurting

Still hurting mentally from yesterday's game, as I hate to be a loser. Just chilled out today, as the missus is working, and I have got to go back to Salisbury refreshed for the game against Woking. On the health front I'm feeling pretty good today, as I'm still taking my tablets, and am getting back to my normal weight, which is always a good sign.

Allow me to digress for a minute as the following incident from my Swansea days is one of the most unusual I have experienced as a professional footballer. We were told there was a meeting with Alan Curtis, who was in temporary charge. It was to inform us that we had been taken over by a multi-millionaire businessman named Tony Petty who was Australia-based, who had acquired shares for £1 (Managing Director Mike Lewis sold them to him). I knew they had just opened the pound shop on the High Street, but this sounded like a joke. It was not long after that we were to find out that the whole thing would be a joke. As we waited in the home dressing room you could feel the tension, and the gossiping had started. Players speculated on who the top players we'd sign would be, who would get new contracts. Little did we know what was to come.

This new chairman was not what I had pictured when he walked into the room. He was no bigger than 5ft 5in, and looked the spitting image of Freddie Mercury. He introduced himself as the 'money guy' and told us that things are looking up. His talk came to an end, and then he decided to drop a bombshell to say the least. 'There are going to be big changes at this club, especially with the squad,' he said. He wanted to speak to fifteen first-team regulars straight away, and named them one by one. I was one of seven players not named, and didn't know what to think. The first player sent in was one of our main players, Matthew Bound. It was not long before he returned with a big smile and the words, 'I've just been sacked.' It was crazy! How could someone turn up and sack one of our best players? Then he continued with several more – turning their careers upside down. In the end he tried to sack eight players, terminate seven more contracts (pay cuts up to 70 per cent of their wages or the option of a free transfer), and sacked Ron Walton as well as our goalkeeping coach, Glan Letheren.

Sacking players, or terminating contracts, was unheard of (and illegal), and just couldn't be done at a Nationwide League club in that manner. Supporters were angered. Thanks to the Nationwide League, sanctions were threatened and our PFA representative Nick Cusack did some wonderful work on the players' behalf (and in November 2001 he replaced Barry Horne as the PFA Chairman). A rival consortium headed by Mel Nurse, a property developer, sought to buyout the new owners. Mel is a former Wales international footballer, who played 257 league games for Swansea in two separate spells between 1955 and 1971. He resigned from the board and the following day bought the club's £801,000 debt.

Did Petty honestly think he was really going to get away going about his business in the manner he tried? Maybe he thought he was Lord Sugar from *The Apprentice*? Ultimately the club managed to avoid going into administration and amid all this turmoil still managed to finish in a healthy mid-table position in the 2001/02 season.

16/2/09 – Speech

I was up early today as I had to head back to Salisbury for training. The first thing we did when we got in was to have a team meeting about Saturday's game, and to talk about tomorrow night's game against Woking. To be honest I'm not a great fan of team meetings, as they can be dragged out and you often find yourself going around in circles. A saying in football is 'we are going to have a meeting about a meeting'. I like a meeting to be short and direct with a manager taking full control, whether you think he's right or wrong. Let's face it – there are too many opinions out there for everyone to wholeheartedly agree on something. For example, when you watch a video of a goal you have given away as a team, every person sees it differently and they see what they want to see. Sometimes you can have too many chiefs, and not enough Indians. But I will say this, there are times when you need meetings in order to benefit the team, and after our previous result we certainly need one. It really was one of the most inspirational speeches I have ever heard. The coach, Tommy Widdrington, spoke from the heart, and it really was just what the doctor ordered. He made a lot of sense, talking about us really digging deep and pulling together as a team together in order to turn our season around. His voice was raised, but not to the point of shouting, and he had a face that looked saddened, but not angered. I believe you can read a lot from someone's facial expressions when they are talking. You could really see that he was hurting, just like we all were, and he knew that there was so much more to come out of those within the four walls. Let's hope it does the trick for tomorrow's game.

17/2/09 Basement Battle

I was feeling good and ready for the basement battle ahead. I chilled out for most of the day, then had my normal one-hour nap – no more, no less. We beat Woking 1–0 and it could have been more. Woking are a strong team, and like us are fighting for their lives. We needed that after last weekend's result. It was so nice to get that winning feeling back, and to top it off I was awarded 'Man of the Match', and a bottle of Salisbury's finest champagne. OK, it was no Moët et Chandon, but it was never going to be consumed anyway as I keep them. My mum prints off stickers to put on the bottles, with the date, the game, and the result on it, so we remember them. I have won close to thirty MOTM awards in my career, which isn't a bad number for a centre-half. It's generally the artists who get the awards, and not the warriors. As a centre-half you would have to score a goal from your own box to get any sort of accolade.

18/2/09 – Bumps

I was in bits after last night's match. Thankfully my parents were at the game so they were able to drive me home. I don't think I would have made it if I was driving alone. They hardly ever miss a game, and are my biggest fans, and that's one of the reasons why I love them so much. I have so many bumps from last night's game. It's just lucky that my blood is getting better as if not, I'd be all the colours of the rainbow today. It was a right old battle which is great for my match fitness.

19/2/09 – Football Tournament

I was so stiff this morning, even more so than yesterday, and I had another journey to Salisbury again. Before training I got a massage from the physio on my calf to get the stiffness out as it was killing me. It's hard to put my foot on the pedal in training as much as I want to, as I was feeling so tight around the groin.

After training Michael Fowler and I went to do some community work. It was for some 'naughty' kids who were having a tournament, to see who could beat each other up first – only joking! It was a football tournament and it was nice to see them so proud of themselves, getting rewards for doing something positive. After it we went back to the digs for some food, with Fowls in charge of the kitchen. He kept his high standards up again, with some steak, potatoes and corn – high living for us footballers. Broughy went out on a date, so for a bit of fun we dressed up in his clothes and kept sending him picture messages to his phone. It's amazing what lads get up to when left to their own devices.

20/2/09 – Summer Baby

I got up nice and early this morning with the sun shining through the window. What a feeling that is after all that bad weather we have had. It's amazing how a bit of sun can really make you buzz – well it works for me! Perhaps it's because I'm a summer baby, born in August. Maybe I should be playing abroad?

Training was short and sharp, just what I like on a Friday, as it really gets you ready for the next day's game. After training the whole squad finished a meeting with a sports psychologist. To be honest, if you asked most footballers what they thought about them they would say that it's all a load of rubbish, but there are some who really make sense. This woman, who works with Doncaster Rovers, was one of them. What she did was a positive in my eyes, and I also think it worked for the rest of the squad. What really impressed me about her was the way she did not impose herself on anyone, and rather let us all open up to her. I've been involved with sports psychologists who were too pushy, and tried to convince everyone that they were 100 per cent right. Footballers hate that sort of attitude, and are very opinionated, so you have to have the ability to work with the believers, and the non-believers.

Tonight I'm on BBC Wales. In recent weeks I have been filming my story so far, from the time I was diagnosed with leukaemia to recovering, and getting back playing again. It has been really enjoyable filming it, and I just hope it comes over the way I'd like it to, and show people that there is always hope. I'm really looking forward to seeing it.

If asked 'are you lucky to be a professional football?' I'd have to answer 'Yes, I am'. In fact, I'd say that every football player is a lucky one because of the lives we lead. We are doing what every man dreams of, and getting paid to do it to boot. Whether it's the lower leagues, the Football League, or in the Premiership we are all the same . . . just with different bank balances and luxuries after training.

When we finish training (for a few hours) I go into town and shop in the likes of Topman and Superdrug, whereas the top players go shopping in Armani and Harrods. On a serious note I believe that every football player is sitting on the periphery of success or failure, as it can only take a very simple change in circumstances to change everything. A bad injury or and illness (like the one I had myself) might see you never play again or recover to your best. Then there's the change of manager where you mightn't be his cup of tea, or on the complete opposite side of the coin you could be the icing on his cake, where he plays you all the time, giving you every opportunity to perform, and when he leaves you leave with him. If just one manager likes you it can really change a player's career.

Over the years I have seen many players disappear from the professional game who had a lot more ability than me, who I genuinely thought would reach the top heights of the game, have all the money in the world, and be a football celebrity. Maybe it's to do with luck or the fifteenth pint they should not have consumed that week, who knows? Luck is a word that is thrown around in football; what I will say, and I'm sure the greats will agree with this, you earn your own luck, and in order to do that you have to make sacrifices. If you asked me what it takes to be a professional footballer I would say this: 30 per cent ability, 60 per cent heart and determination, and 10 per cent luck.

21/2/09 – Away Game

Woke up in bits, but I must tell myself differently as we have a really tough away match at Crawley Town. They have been playing well and are going for the play-offs. We left this morning by bus, on my first away trip with the new lads. Like at Torquay, the banter was second to none. We played cards, and yes, I lost again. New team – but the same luck with the cards. The result was a great one for both Salisbury and Torquay, as we beat Crawley 3–0. Another clean sheet to boot, and I feel I'm getting back to my very best. After the game I went to James' fight, which he won in front of a large crowd of people, including Joe Calzaghe and Nicky Piper (Cardiff-born and the former Commonwealth light heavyweight champion). I'm so happy for my little brother, and I really think he has a huge future ahead of him.

22/2/09 – Winning

After the fight last night we went into Cardiff with a few of our Cullompton mates to go clubbing. It was the first time I have ever been to Cardiff for a night out, and it really lived up to what I had heard about it. It's always good to have friends outside of those involved in football, as it allows you to get away from the football world. Of course it's different when you have a bad result – nothing lifts you from that. I actually wasn't feeling too bad when I woke up this morning, and thought I'd have been in a worse state. I hadn't been home since Wednesday so it was nice to see my two girls. I seem to be away from home all the time, and when I am, I miss them so much.

People often ask me what I was like at school. Let's just say that I was like a fish out of water. I never really could find my feet in school and spent more time outside the classroom than in it. I think this was due to not being academic and having only one vision. I have to admit though, that when I did go to lessons I enjoyed them, and excelled with anything to do with my hands, like art, woodwork and metalwork. Funny that, as these were the only results I had when I left school, with two passes in woodwork and metalwork, and a full GCSE B in art. As the final years approached my mum and dad sat down the Penlan School Headmaster John Guy. They informed him that Swansea were willing to let me train with them as a work experience lad. It was going to be more beneficial for me to train with them three times a week as it was going to give me a better chance of becoming a footballer. This turned out to be the best decision for me personally, and my career, thanks in a large part to my parents and the school.

23/2/09 – Back in Training

I'm back in Devon for training today with Torquay, something that I haven't done for some time, so I was a little worried, but it was great to catch up with the lads again. I had a chat with the gaffer about what's going to happen when my loan finishes with Salisbury. He said good things, but not the sort of things I wanted to hear.

He said he knew I'd been doing well at Salisbury but that he couldn't guarantee that I'd be coming straight back into the team. He said that if the lads do well in the next two games then he wasn't going to change the team. So it was really just a matter of waiting. I'm coming back for sure, not because I haven't enjoyed my time at Salisbury – it's been a really good experience – but Torquay United are my team.

After training Amylia and I headed down to Exmouth beach for a walk and an ice cream, which gave Gemma some time to herself. Picture me going down to Exmouth with £3, using it to buy some chips and ice cream for us, then getting 20p change before settling down to eat the chips. After that I said to Amylia, 'Will we have our ice cream?' The next thing was that everything went completely wrong as I opened the wrapper. I dropped the ice cream and had no money to buy another one – what a dope! And to top it off there was a family standing next to us, which included a little boy watching us. He must have thought, 'how tight's this guy?', as I pushed Amylia quickly away on her little bike unable to buy another one for her.

24/2/09 – New Baby

We went to the hospital today to find out how the new baby is doing. Gemma hasn't been feeling too good lately. It's been such a worry over the last few days as she has been bleeding quite a lot. I must say that what's been going on really scares me. I don't show it though as I have got to show her that I'm strong. We went, and got great news. They scanned the baby and everything was fine. After having so much worry, to see the little one on the scan with a strong heartbeat . . . I nearly broke down.

As I've said before, I am a big softie at heart. Afterwards I went to watch Torquay playing Forest Green. It wasn't the best result as we drew 3–3 but on the other hand it was a very entertaining game. Maybe they need a strong Welshman back in the side.

25/2/09 – Boxing

Our usual Wednesday off was cancelled after last night's bad result, so the gaffer brought the lads in to do warm-down. I wasn't complaining though as I hadn't trained much this week because of a tight hamstring. It was nice to do a bit with the team, and then a bit extra with the lads who didn't play the night before. After training I went to the gym for some weights, but got dragged into some boxing with Lee Mansell and Kevin Nicholson. I hadn't boxed for a long time, but really enjoyed getting back into it. I bet I'll feel it tomorrow though when I wake up. If you ever want to get fit, I'm telling you now that boxing is a good sport to do.

Fighting has always been in my blood as you would expect, as I have three brothers. Whether it was boxing or wrestling that's all we did. We used to have 'Royal Rumbles' daily, and my mum would be pulling her hair out screaming at us to stop. But how was that going to work when my dad was the main culprit, always starting it? Of course they were play-fights, but sometimes they would boil over to full-on fights that would not look out of place in the UFC. So the love for boxing has always been there, but being a footballer it's very hard to fit the two sports together. The only time I really get the chance to get my fists moving is in the close season where I get right stuck into training and sparring like a full-time boxer. Maybe one day I will get the chance to fight in a real bout.

The lads are playing Cullompton in the Devon Bowl tonight. But I think I'll give it a miss, as the Champions League is on the box. Real Madrid or Cullompton? Sorry lads.

26/3/09 – Back Training

We had another round with the psychologist today. This time we got talking about professional athletes, and we were asked to give some names of athletes and talk about their lifestyles. Well, what can I say – it turned into a full-blown debate. We talked about drinking, eating and smoking, and if they did these things, can they be classed as true professionals? Some said they were. Some disagreed. But how can you decide? When asked to name some names the lads came out with two of the best football players who lived – Maradona and George Best, and we all know how they lived their lives. Call them professional athletes? What I will say though is that every person knows his/her individual body, and if you can perform to your highest standard possible having fun (and it's legal), then why not?

27/3/09 – North Wales

I'm on my travels again with Salisbury for our game against Wrexham on Saturday. Having had to come up a day before it's made it one hell of a journey. On our way we stopped at Port Vale's training ground to do some training. They had a great set-up and training facilities, especially for a League 2 outfit. After training we went to our hotel and it really was a top hotel. I have stayed in plenty over the years for football – some good, some bad.

But I always have, and always will, remember this one hotel called the Floatel, where I stayed when with Exeter. Not a word of a lie, it was floating on water – shocking. There were even life jackets all around the hallways. It was like Fawlty Towers but on water, and rocking side to side. That's what you get for living the life of a superstar. It's a big game tomorrow, and it would be nice if we could get something not only for ourselves, but also for Torquay.

28/3/09 – Good Sleep

Great sleep as the curtains totally black out the whole room. It's some contrast to our digs in Salisbury that don't have any. The game went to plan, and we came away with a super point that could have been all three on another day. After the game I got to do a duet with Dean Saunders, my dad's cousin, on BBC Wales. He gave me a big lift as well by saying that I had done really well in the game. It was a real family affair, with my parents, Dean and his wife Helen, all chatting away.

It was a long trip home after the match, but the point had us on a high. I think we sang all the way back. Got home at around 11.30 p.m. and then it was get in, get ready as fast as possible, and out. Can you imagine what we would have been like had we won?

1/3/09 – Carlsberg Wife

After yesterday's game and the night's antics I was, as you can imagine, exhausted today. My 'Carlsberg wife' was so good to me again, as she said that considering we have a game on Tuesday it would be silly to drive back just for one day. She really is the best wife ever. In the afternoon a few of us went to Pizza Hut, and then on to the cinema to see *Slumdog Millionaire*. The film really lived up to the hype and the acting was second-to-none. It was amazing to see the way other people live their lives, and it makes you aware of how lucky you are. It also goes to show just how much talent there is out there if you just go and look for it.

2/3/09 – Making my Mind Up

Nick Holmes, the Salisbury manager, asked me today if I wanted to stay on with them for another month. He had spoken to Bucks who told him that it would be fine for me to stay, as long as there was a 24-hour call-back in the loan period. I'm not sure what to do to be honest. It's a good thing that Salisbury want me to stay, but on the other hand the gaffer is showing no sign at the moment of bringing me back. That's a big disappointment, but I can see his problem as the lads are playing so well. I just need to keep my head down, work away, and wait for my chance.

My main aim is to return to Torquay. I'm not sure if I should stay, and asked Nick if I could let him know after the game. But if it's going to keep me playing then I may as well stay on.

3/3/09 – Game Off

I was looking forward to tonight's game. I went into town for some afternoon tea and a sandwich, and then went back to have my afternoon kip. When I woke up from that I had my pre-match meal of egg on toast, and went to the game on a real high ready for battle. I was hit with a blow though as the ref went on to the pitch to check if it was playable. Personally, I would have played the game but he called it off. Sometimes you have to wonder if it's down to the ref just not fancying it himself? Bit cold. Bit wet. Who knows? Disappointed to say the least.

4/3/09 – Brother's Birthday

I was back in Devon today after last night's game was called off, and it was nice to get woken up by my little princess, Amylia. Later in the day I waited for my brothers to arrive as they were down to have bone marrow tests (to see if they match mine, as I may need a bone marrow transplant in the future). It was a nightmare to be honest, as they couldn't do them today because they had nothing arranged. It was probably down to them not contacting me to ask whether they were still coming down. What a mess. Maybe I should have phoned them, but things have just been so hectic. Not to worry though, as we found out they can have it done in Swansea, so they won't have to travel to Devon again for it. It wasn't a completely wasted journey for them though as we headed out to celebrate James' 21st birthday in Exmouth.

I also had a chat with Dr Roberts about my blood, which is spot-on. He and his team have been brilliant and I am so grateful to them all. I was brought down to earth a bit as we talked about what the next stage was, as my blood is starting to get back to normal. I had more blood taken today to find out how many bad blood cells I have left, and if I'm still producing them then there are other things that may need to be done. But one things that stood out was that a bone marrow transplant might someday have to take place to clear this terrible disease.

5/3/09 – Taxi Driver

Well we had a great night In Exmouth for James' birthday and even managed to get a taxi back home for £30 which is class as it is a right trek. Luckily I know the driver – Dave, a Torquay fan, who lives in Exmouth. We did have some fun with him on the way home as it took forever. Then it started snowing really badly and we were lucky to get back to Cullompton. We were saying on the way that his taxi was a 'Carlsberg taxi', just having a bit of craic with him. He was effing and blinding saying it was a joke price, and that he would have to drive all the way back to Exmouth in the snow. Anyway, thanks Dave.

I went for a 20-minute run today, as I was not in training. When I got home I took Amylia to the park. She really had fun and it was so nice spending quality time with her. The rest of the day was spent chilling out and catching up with some sleep. Back to Salisbury tomorrow to get ready for the weekend's game against Kidderminster.

6/3/09 – The Express

I drove to Salisbury on my own this morning, as I was off yesterday, and all those in the car school were already there. How I got there on my own I'll never know, as every time I have travelled with the lads in the past I have talked all the way, taking no notice of the journey. It was good to see all the lads again, and have a bit of banter with them. As soon as I walked in I noticed there was a picture hanging on my peg, of a look-a-like. It looked nothing like me, but hey, it was good for morale. I have given the lads so much stick that a bit back won't hurt.

We watched a film tonight called *The Express*, about a young African-American American football player called Ernie Davis who battled all his life to become a professional player. He turned out to be a top player, and was the first African-American to win the Heisman Trophy, which was given to the Most Valuable Player in collegiate football. The film explores civil topics, such as racism, discrimination and athletics. The reason the film had such an impact on me was that Davis' career was suddenly stopped in its tracks when he was diagnosed with leukaemia, and could no longer play. When he became a professional athlete in the NFL in 1962, he signed for the Cleveland Browns, had a number of health concerns, and tests showed that he had leukaemia. Like me he called a press conference to tell the world about his condition and that he wouldn't be playing for the foreseeable future.

A few weeks after his diagnosis, Davis, in full uniform, led his team out on to the pitch as a fitting tribute to him – something of course which I can empathise with. He sadly died a year later, aged just 23. It was surreal watching it, and was one of the most moving films I have ever watched. It had a real meaning to me and it makes me think how lucky I am to be still playing. It's well worth a watch.

7/3/09 – Missed Penalty

We got a good 0–0 draw against Kidderminster today, but it could have been even better had we scored a last-minute penalty. It was a good point as Kidderminster are in the promotion places, and it was also our third clean sheet in four games.

Michael Brough and I have a really good partnership going at the moment. After the game we drove home to

Swansea for my brother James' late 21st birthday party. It was a great night, enjoyed by all, and Michael got a proper Welsh welcome from my family. It was a right laugh all round, and it was good to catch up with friends and family.

8/3/09 – Towers

After a great night last night it was so nice to wake up next to my wife. It was just the two of us as Amylia was home in Devon with Gemma's parents. We stayed in a really nice hotel called the Towers, and managed to get up in time to have a great hotel breakfast. After that we went into town to do a bit of shopping, and on our return we used the spa pool. That evening we went for a Welsh roast at my mum's – your mum's food is always the best. Then it was back to Devon to watch our wedding video.

I also received a phone call from Bucks to say that I wasn't forgotten about at Torquay. That was a great feeling as it showed that I was still in his plans, and even though I'm enjoying my time at Salisbury, I want to return to Torquay and regain my place in the starting XI as soon as possible.

9/3/09 – Still on Loan

I spent the day in Salisbury after travelling up this morning. I'm still on loan, and getting games, which is vitally important for me. Training was good, and after it we had a small meeting with the squad and Tommy Widdrington, who had some nice comments about the Torquay lads by saying that we showed the same level of commitment, and trained with the same intensity as in matches. I have always trained hard and have always thought that you should train the way you play. This evening I cooked for the lads, the best chicken pasta ever, which I made from scratch. I was well chuffed with myself – watch out Jamie Oliver!

10/3/09 – Curry and Chips

We were away to Weymouth tonight, in what was a big relegation 6-pointer. It's completely different here than at Torquay, as we have to drive to games in cars. The lads at Torquay don't know how lucky they are. It wasn't too bad though as Weymouth is on the way home to Devon. We needed the win, and got it in comprehensive fashion, winning 4–0. I scored the opening goal, and it really was a great feeling to get back on the goal trail. Even though I've been a defender for the whole of my professional career I've been known to pop up with a goal every now and again. To be honest the first 30 minutes was tough as they have a lot of young players who worked extremely hard, but we matched them, and after the first goal we settled down and dominated the rest of the match – a good three points. After the game I stopped for a curry and chips by the roadside . . . just like the Premiership stars?

11/3/09 – Saint

Not a lot going on today. There's no training due to last night's game so I just spent some time with the family. I took Amylia for a walk to the park to get the stiffness out of my legs, but also to give Gemma some peace and quiet. She really needs it at the minute with me away all the time. It must be really hard work looking after Amylia, considering she's pregnant, and to top it off she is so worried about her dad as he is due to have major surgery soon. She's a saint really.

12/3/09 - More Filming

We had Setanta around today to do more filming, following on from the last time. This time it would show me back playing, and generally just enjoying life again. It's amazing that Amylia has been on TV more times than most people will ever be, and she doesn't even have a clue!

I tried to sort out some stuff to do with our car as we think that we'll need a bigger one, especially with another little one on the way. It's so disappointing that we have only had the car a year, and it's already lost about £1,500 of its value. Cars . . .

13/3/09 - Friday the 13th

Today was Friday the 13th, and as we all know, it's meant to be a day of bad luck. I have to say it wasn't for me today – my mum rang me to say she was after entering me into a modelling competition (as you do), to be the face of the new men's clothing shop, Slaters, which was opening soon in Swansea. I only got a call to say that I'm in the last 15!

That night we watched Red Nose Day on TV. It's so uplifting, seeing so many people raising so much money. It just goes to show that if you make people aware then they will help. It's all about awareness and getting your message out to the public.

14/3/09 - Big Task

We had a big task today as we were playing the league leaders Burton away. Incredibly the bookies have already paid out on them as champions. Recently they have lost a couple of games, and the way we are playing I really did think that we had a big chance of getting all 3 points. I was right as we won 2–1, which has obviously blown a massive hole in their title hopes, giving other teams more than a glimmer of hope of catching them, including, most importantly, ourselves. Everyone thought it was over, but who knows what will happen now?

I got home to watch two big boxing fights, one that featured my mate Enzo Maccarinelli. It was a must-win fight for him tonight, as he needed to get his title hopes back on track. I can't believe I'm writing this but he got knocked out – what a shock!

I couldn't find my tablets tonight as I only had one left! I'm hoping that I'll be able to collect my full three-month prescription tomorrow, as I'm not sure if the hospital pharmacy will be open. One day of not taking my tablet won't hurt. Two nights though? That would be pushing it.

15/3/09 - Lucky

Today was the first chance I've had to visit Brian in hospital, and I took Amylia with me to try to cheer him up. He was in good form, which is good news for the family. Hopefully in another week or two he'll be back on his feet. Lucky old me – went to get the tablets and the hospital pharmacy was open. We had some food in town and then I took one straight away as that's what the doctor told me to do if there was ever a problem. So it wasn't too bad, as I was worried that the place was going to be closed . . . that would have left me in big trouble as tomorrow I return to Salisbury.

16/3/09 – Playing Friday

Good news about Brian today – he's feeling a lot better. It must be because he saw me yesterday! Tomorrow night we've a tough game against Eastbourne. I always enjoy playing at night as you get to rest up for the day. There's just something different about playing a game at night. When I was playing for Drogheda United in Ireland, they always played their league games on a Friday night under floodlights. I always thought that it was a great idea, as if you had a family, you had plenty of time to spend with them. I personally think we would have better crowds coming to our matches if we did that here, as a lot of fans play football themselves on Saturdays, so playing on Friday nights would give them the opportunity to come and see us while still having the chance to play their own games. The FA should really look into this for the lower leagues especially.

17/3/09 – Tough Game

We had another tough game tonight, drawing 0–0 against a decent Eastbourne outfit. The game was played in windy conditions, and was a right old scrap, but they're the type of games I love. Before the game we would have taken a point, and overall it was a good night as we kept a clean sheet, and Torquay's assistant Shaun North was there. My performance tonight did me no harm in terms of going back to Torquay, and hopefully regaining my place in the starting XI. I need to get back there for the big promotion push!

18/3/09 – Family Visit

We got back this morning at 'silly o'clock' having travelled back from Eastbourne. I was lucky that Gemma told me that I could have a nice lie-in this morning, as I needed it badly. Eventually I decided to go into town with the family to do some shopping. Tonight my cousin, Sarah Hutchings, was down from Swansea with Eva (her daughter) and her boyfriend Nicky. It's always nice having friends and family coming down to stay. It brings a nice Welsh touch to Devon.

19/3/09 – Returning Home

I woke up on a fine Thursday morning to the noise of two babies, which will become a normal occurrence for me soon with our second one on the way. Gem's dad came out of hospital today, which is the news we were all hoping for. As if that wasn't good enough news I got some myself, which was the news that I was waiting for – it was a call from Torquay to say that I was being called back. I must say, I'm going to miss Salisbury very much. I have met and worked with some super people, and their fans always show great support. It has been a real pleasure playing here, and I cannot thank them enough for the opportunity to get back playing again. It's a club full of potential, with good management, and a ground that can be built on. There are some great players on their books who could do a job for Torquay; the likes of Mike Fowler, Rob Sinclair and Charlie Griffin especially.

I thought I would be travelling with Torquay to Northwich tomorrow morning after training, but there was one final twist to come! Even my return was not simple. Colin Lee, Torquay United's Director of Football, had called to say I would be receiving a call from the gaffer, Paul Buckle, to confirm my recall later that day. But the Salisbury lads wanted the final say . . . between Michael Fowler and the Salisbury Chairman they decided to get me back by having their final joke, saying Salisbury were going to retain my registration and stop my return. My return gone in one phone call! . . . or so I thought. I was caught hook, line and sinker! It was not until I heard the laughing on the other end of the phone line that I realised it was a joke. I guess what goes around comes around.

20/3/09 – Car School

I got back into the swing of things nice and early today by way of the car school with Martin Rice and Greavsey. I have missed the long chats about dogs with Ricey and of course Greavsey's bad jokes. I walked into a lot of smiles and greetings, which is always nice. It was the first time I've trained with the lads at Torquay for quite some time. We worked on our shape for tomorrow's game against Northwich, and I'm hoping that I will get back into the starting XI. I simply can't wait to get my old number 6 shirt back on again. What a nice start back . . . as we have a massive journey of around 6 or 7 hours ahead, of bad jokes and looking at Mustapha Carayol's ugly mug and massive DJ earphones across the table.

21/3/09 – Different Bed

Another night and a different bed. That sounds quite bad, haha! We stayed at the Ramada Jarvis in Manchester, getting ready for today's game. I didn't have the best sleep as it was too hot and the bed was rubbish. Other than that I was really looking forward to my first game in a Torquay shirt for some time.

We didn't start the game well, found ourselves 1–0 down at half time, and were under a lot of pressure from a big, strong side. An inspiring half-time talk from the management though, and everything changed. I got my first goal of the season in the yellow of Torquay and what a buzz! I couldn't believe how it happened. Sometimes I think I see things before they happen. In my sleep last night I was dreaming of scoring today.

It went something like this: Tim Sills had a header parried by the keeper, it fell in front of me and from 3 yards out I buried it. It felt as good as a 30-yard volley. I couldn't have planned it better. It really is the best goal I've ever scored, all things considered.

Having drawn back level, we managed to give them another goal back. I always had the feeling though that we would get back in it, and if we drew level again I knew we would go on to win. Tim Sills scored from a header, and once we drew level again we were the better team. From a long throw-in Roscoe smashed another goal home. It was a massive win, and my return couldn't have turned out better.

The downside to living in sunny Devon are the long trips home . . . but at least when you win it makes it easier.

22/3/09 – Gardening

I was hoping to make Gemma breakfast in bed today, but woke up after her, so obviously that didn't happen! Yesterday's game took it out of me, and to top it off Gemma had to go to work. So Amylia and I went for a walk to see her in action and to have a coffee. On the way back I dropped Amylia off at Nanny Howarth's so I could have some time on my own to do the garden – Gem has been on to me about it for so long. It took me some time as you can imagine, as I haven't cut it in months – and I mean months. It looked like a jungle, but I eventually got it all sorted, and it looks pretty good. You'd have sworn Charlie Dimmock had been waving her magic bits around it. When Gemma got home from work we all went to Gem's parents' house for a Mother's Day lunch. It was brilliant to see Brian up and about again.

23/3/09 – Scratchcards

Another crucial game against Grays tomorrow, so we were back in Newton Abbot today for training, and the games are really coming at us thick and fast. It's going to be a very interesting few weeks as there are not a lot of games left until the end of the season, and with so much to play for, who knows what will happen?

Other than training not a lot happened today, apart from when I went into a shop today to get something for dinner. I went to the till to pay, but fancied a flutter so I asked the cashier if I could have a £100,000 scratchcard. Well if you could have seen his face – he was gobsmacked. I repeated my request, '£100,000 scratchcard, please.' He thought I wanted 100,000 scratchcards. It's Torquay United I play for, not Manchester United.

24/3/09 – Home Return

Today was my first home game at Plainmoor since back in December, so I tried to chill out for the day. I went for lunch with the missus and a spot of shopping.

I received a great reception from the crowd at the match. There were banners all around the ground, and the way I felt when I saw it is a feeling I will never forget. The fans have been really brilliant. When the game started, things didn't go to plan as we fell a goal behind. Like during the half time of our previous game, the gaffer had a few choice words to say to us, and the match finished 1–1. Not a bad point I suppose, but it would have been so much better for me personally if I had managed to get a head on a great cross towards the end of the match. Unfortunately I just missed it. Maybe I'm not meant to be hero yet.

25/3/09 – Balloons

It's Gem's birthday tomorrow so I popped into town to get a few things. I find it hard to buy for her so just got things like balloons and banners. I did say to her that I would take her to town to buy some clothes, but she has everything. Before I went to bed I stuck all the balloons and banners up, so that when she gets up she'll get a nice surprise. I'm a big softie really.

26/3/09 – Birthday Wishes

Well Gemma turned 25, and she had to get up early on her own to go to work. It was only 3 hours' work though. She was very well happy with what I had done for her. After work she opened all her presents and then I headed off to training. When I came back it was a quick change, and then up the motorway to Swansea. We were going there to have some suit fittings for the 'Face of Slater's' catwalk. I still think they were trying to suss me out! My parents took Amylia for the night, while Gem and I had an Indian.

27/3/09 – New Signing

I had to leave early this morning to make it into training. I try to treat every training session as if I was playing a match, and had a great tussle with Matt Green throughout. I like it when that happens as it gets you into the zone. The bus journey to Mansfield was the same as usual, other than I was looking across at our new signing Blair Sturrock, who had signed from Swindon Town on loan. Hopefully he'll give us an extra edge, and help push us to promotion.

On the health front I'm feeling good in myself, but I've still not received any results from the other week, so I can only guess everything's alright!

28/3/09 – Good Point

We stayed in a nice hotel about an hour's drive from Mansfield, which had some really beautiful gardens. I had an early breakfast and then went for a morning walk around them, which has inspired me to do my own little garden when I get back.

In the match the same pattern continued as we went 1–0 down, and then came back to draw 1–1 with Blair scoring the goal. So he's made an impact already. We're still in the play-offs after this result, and are showing some real steel in our matches, and a great desire to boot. Everyone's working for one another, and if we keep this up we'll hopefully start turning these draws into wins.

29/3/09 – Time Off

The gaffer has given us three days off, so as of yesterday I am doing the garden. I started at midday, and didn't finish it until the evening time. I didn't even have a break, as once I start to do something I have to finish it as soon as possible. It looks like a show house garden, even if I do say so myself.

I got the test results back today and it was great news. The doctor said that the results were as good as I could have hoped for, and that I'm only producing 0.62 bad molecular blood cells. To celebrate we went for a drink and some food with Wayne and Emma in Exeter.

30/3/09 – Gardening Again

More gardening today and I'm really getting into it now. Went into Homebase to buy some plants that cost around £50. I couldn't believe a few shrubs could cost so much. I may have to put this gardening on hold for a bit because of the credit crunch! I've actually found it all so peaceful, allowing me to gather my thoughts, and fall into the world of a gardener. It's left me with some muscle pains though, which I wasn't expecting. I really do feel sorry for gardeners all over . . . and especially the older generation.

31/3/09 – Biggest Supporter

I feel really recharged for the run-in now, following the three days off. I had a phone call today from the modelling competition people, saying that I have got to be there tomorrow at 5.30 p.m., and ready for the catwalk at 6.00 p.m. After that we'll find out who is the overall winner. She did say that I have a lot of votes, and there was one person who had voted a lot. Well I laughed, knowing of course that it could only have been my biggest supporter . . . my mum!

1/4/09 – Winner

It was great to have so much support from the family at Slater's today. There was a large crowd in attendance, with some famous Welsh rugby stars, and a Miss Wales who I thought was fit, but not worldly . . . I would have Gem any day of the week over her. I enjoyed the walk on the catwalk, and when the result was announced I couldn't believe it. 'The winner is Chris Todd!' – I nearly fell over. I am now £1,000 richer with vouchers to spend in the shop, and am the face of Slater's. To celebrate I spent £700 of the vouchers on my dad, brothers, grandparents . . . and something for me of course.

2/4/09 – Buzzing

I got home very late last night, but to be honest I'm still on a high after the result. I went to training and when I told the lads about me winning, they gave me a fair bit of stick (which I was expecting). They were saying it was a fix, that it must have been a balaclava-modelling competition, that I paid them, or they felt sorry for me.

I was back in hospital today, and not for the reason I am normally there. I took another whack on the foot I hurt a few weeks back, so I was in a lot of pain and needed an x-ray to make sure there was no break. The good news is that there isn't any break – it's just badly bruised.

3/4/09 - Face of Slater's

What a fine and sunny Devon morning! In for training, ready for the big match against Kettering, but we didn't do too much so we would be as fresh as possible for tomorrow. The team was named today. It's great when you get some notice as you can prepare yourself psychologically, but it's not too great when you're not in the team, which I've experienced myself, as it makes you lose some of your focus.

I'm officially a model now, as I was in the *South Wales Evening Post* for winning the 'Face of Slater's'. I was also in the *Sun*, but didn't make page 3.

4/4/09 - Easter Weekend

Today was the start of two massive games in the space of three days over Easter. It's a real test for players, playing games so close together, and you really need to be on your game. We had a good start to the weekend, played really well and won 2–0 against Kettering Town, one of our play-off rivals. Then, if that wasn't enough, all the results went our way today as the teams battling with us in the play-offs lost, including Stevenage, Histon and Cambridge. The best result though was that league leaders Burton lost 4–0 to Crawley. That result just might have opened the door for us to win the league. And remember, we play them on Monday night.

5/4/09 - Day Early

We were in training early today, so that we could be in and out and prepared early for our match again Burton, which will be live on Setanta Sports tomorrow night. I turned up thinking we were travelling, and had my tracksuit on. There was only one problem . . . we aren't travelling until tomorrow. It was Gemma who told me that we were travelling today. I don't know if she just wanted to get rid of me a day early, but the lads got a good laugh out of it. Ah, sure if I can help with the morale then I don't mind, haha! If we get the right result tomorrow we would be ever so close to winning the league.

6/4/09 — Service Break

We travelled to the game this afternoon and it was going well until we had a pit stop. We got back on the bus, went down the motorway, and then there were fits of laughter from the front of the bus. We'd only gone and left physio Peter Morgan behind! We had to drive to the next junction, turn around and pick him up, adding another half an hour to the journey. In fairness, he took it in good spirits. As if that wasn't enough the bus driver only went and missed the junction for where we were getting our pre-match meal. If it were not for Kevin Nicholson and Tim Sills being switched on he would have kept going up the motorway, which would have been a disaster for us. Finally we got there, and had our pre-match food an hour late. So it wasn't exactly the best of starts to our evening.

After such a shocking start to the day you would have thought it might have had some sort of an effect on our performance against the league leaders. We went out and won 1–0 in good style, with Danny Stevens scoring an excellent goal. It's just what we needed to keep the dream alive. We are now just 8 points behind with a game in hand, and there are four games in total left, including having to play Burton in the final game. All we can do now is win our games and see what happens. Burton's form has been falling away ever since Nigel Clough's departure to Derby County. We must still have a chance?

7/4/09 – Match Replay

We had the day off today after last night's late return (we'd got in at around 3.00 a.m.). I did some more shopping, and then returned to watch last night's game. It was a good performance all round. I fancy us at the moment for promotion, but obviously I don't want to speak too soon. All of our promotion rivals had poor results, which are always nice to hear about.

A footnote on the car situation – never buy a brand new one on finance, as you'll lose so much money. I found this out to my cost today. We are thinking of changing ours after one year, and have lost the best part of £3,000, not £1,500 as we previously thought. I feel sick . . . and it's nothing to do with the leukaemia.

8/4/09 – Another Missed Tablet

Surprise, surprise . . . I forgot to take my tablet today. I think that's the third time I have now forgotten, so have decided to set a reminder on my phone. We had the day off today to recharge the batteries, and make sure we're ready for the weekend's game against Crawley. The right result will push us closer to the title.

We don't fear anyone at the moment, and having a rest like this is an important part of the jigsaw when you are playing games so close together. I went to look at a BMW today, but this time took Gemma's dad to inspect it with me, as he deals in cars. I didn't end up buying it due to the fact that they were only offering peanuts for the Clio. As it's still on finance we'd be taking a huge loss on it, so we are now trying to sell it privately. Hopefully we will get a little more money, and then start again with a loan rather than finance.

9/4/09 – Backroom Staff

A familiar face was at training today – my old centre-half partner Broughy, who has been called back from Salisbury for our run-in, and could have a key part to play. After training I had to get some treatment on my ankle, which involved an ultrasound, ice and a massage. The backroom staff are so important to the players at any football club. I had a good session in the gym afterwards. It's like an Olympic competition in there, and it's usually myself, Greavsey, Scott Bevan, Mansell and Greeny – all the lads have their tops off, and it's a case of 'let's see who can get the most ripped'. I got home and Gemma had dyed her hair dark brown. It's not normally what I go for. I'm a blonde man, but can't divorce her for it. Only kidding – she looks great!

10/4/09 – Jeans

It's amazing what stick you get for just wearing something different. Today I wore my stonewash jeans that are back 'in' for the summer. Well I got hammered for them . . . why, I do not know. They were saying they were old! But I think they really loved them, and were only jealous.

Everyone was buzzing in training today, ready for another tough game against Crawley. There are some big games in the league tomorrow, including the crucial clash between Burton and Histon. We really need Histon to get something from that game to give us a chance of lifting the title. But we'll have to put that game to one side, and just concentrate on our own against Crawley.

I got out the banners and balloons ready for tomorrow as it's Amylia's first birthday. It's unreal to think just how quickly the year has gone by, and what we've all gone through professionally, but most importantly personally. It's been quite eventful to say the least.

My brother, Thomas, kept up the good name of Todd tonight as he won his first amateur boxing match, although I think he needs to hang up his gloves now while the going is good. It would be great to finish 1 and 0.

11/4/09 – Disappointed

It was great singing 'Happy Birthday' to Amylia, and watching her open all her presents and cards. The back garden is just full of toys.

I was feeling really positive about the game against Crawley today. I knew it was going to be a tough game, but I thought we would have enough to win, and keep fighting for the title. How wrong was I? We played poorly today, which was really surprising. There's an old saying – 'after the Lord Mayor's Show', which means you've suffered an anti-climax, and that was just how I would describe the game today. We lost 2–0, but still had three really good chances.

Is the title dream over? Probably, as Burton beat Histon, but the dream of getting promoted is still alive. Today's result may just turn out to be a blessing in disguise in the long run. Who knows? If we had gone right to the wire, and then missed out on the title, it may have spoilt our play-off hopes. Now we must concentrate on getting into the play-offs, and most importantly winning them!

12/4/09 – Birthday

We were in for a cool-down today following yesterday's game. This afternoon I went out for a drive with Amylia in my parents' car as they were down again. By now they must have done more miles than the Concorde. We went out for a few hours which was good for Gemma as she was able to crack on sorting stuff for Amylia's birthday party. The place looked amazing, and what a spread. It was an excellent day. Some of the lads were around, and it was nice for everyone to get their minds off yesterday's game. I'm looking forward to another big game tomorrow against my former team Salisbury. It's going to be nice to go back and see the players and fans. As soon as it kicks off, though, it will be straight down to business. We need the 3 points to secure our play-off spot. And after Saturday's result we need a performance.

13/4/09 – Salisbury

My return to Salisbury was so special. What a greeting I received from the fans, who were coming up hugging and kissing me. The lads at Torquay couldn't believe how nice people were being. Greavsey said was it as if I'd been playing there for 10 years, and not just a few months.

The game itself didn't go as planned. We had three penalties and only scored one. The game ended in a 2–2 draw, and in the end we were lucky as Broughy got sent off with 15 minutes left when we were down 2–1. But then after that we still managed to equalise through

Nicky Wroe. It was a crazy game, with some terrible refereeing. Both sets of fans showed me great support, singing my name, and giving me a great round of applause on the way off. We're still in the play-off places, but it's getting really tight. We need a few more points to be sure. It's mad to think that just two games earlier we were going for the title and now we're fighting to stay in a play-off place.

14/4/09 - Meetings

After the game the gaffer went mad, and told us that the only place we were going to sort our form out was on the training field. So this morning we were all in, which was unusual as we normally have the day off after a game. We had group meetings, divided into our positions, but as the defenders and midfielders took so long, the strikers didn't get in to have their chat! I'm not going to get into what was said. All I'll say is that there were a lot of home truths told in those meetings. It's best to clear the air sometimes.

15/4/09 - Terrible Ones

We were off today, something which I think we needed after the last few days, so I did what I do best when I'm off, which is to chill out and spend time with my angel Amylia. I think that's the first time I have called her that. You often hear of the 'terrible twos', but I didn't think kids have 'terrible ones' as well! Amylia is everywhere, opening cupboards and pulling everything out, destroying the house, wanting everything she's not meant to have, and worst of all, turning off the TV when you're trying to watch something. To calm her down I took her to the swimming pool in Tiverton, and she loved every minute of it. It's just so important to take advantage of your day off, and it's great to have a family as they are always there to take your mind off what's happening on the pitch.

16/4/09 – Sing-Song

We trained at Plainmoor today instead of at our training ground at Newton Abbot racecourse, which is at times never fit for the horses, let alone us. We worked on a solid 4-4-2 shape for the Stevenage match, which is a formation I agree with and really enjoy playing in. I went into Exmouth after training, as it was such a nice evening.

We went to the jungle gym on the front, and onto the beach and Amylia loved every minute of it. The sea air really knocked her for six so I had to try to keep her awake until we got home so I could give her a bath. So what's the best way to do that? Obviously, to sing! I sang to her all the way home, all the top tunes like 'The wheels on the bus' and 'Old McDonald' . . . poor thing.

17/4/09 – Yellow Bus

You should have seen the state of the bus we got on to go to the Stevenage match, which is a huge game for us. It was a big, ugly, yellow one with no electrics and the worst seats ever. What made it even worse is that we were stuck in all sorts of traffic the whole way down. One downside in a footballer's life is the travelling. It's a shame we are not sponsored by Flybe, like we were when I was with Exeter – we used to fly to most of the away games up north like York, Morecambe, etc. I actually can't remember losing a game when travelling by air in style. Maybe Flybe should strike a deal with all the Devon clubs.

Having said that, you would think that travelling long distances all the time would take its toll over a season, but our away record has been quite good, and one of the building blocks for our fine league form and current position. We have 11 wins, 4 draws and just the 4 defeats away from Plainmoor, which is an excellent record. Let's hope it will carry on for the remainder of the season and see us all the way to Wembley.

18/4/09 – Sleep

I must have slept for 10 hours solid last night. I think I might have to change the bed at home as the one in the hotel was hard, while ours is soft. I always thought that today was going to be tough, so I wasn't too disappointed that we drew 0–0, especially as we had Lee Mansell sent off with 30 minutes left. We dug in, and got a well-earned point which could make a huge difference by the end of the season.

We could even have had all three points, had the ref not pulled me up for a perfect goal that he disallowed for a foul that only he saw. And you wonder why footballers get frustrated with refs sometimes?

19/4/09 – Winter Swimming

We had a day off today so I thought it would be in my interests to go and put my skinny legs in the great blue sea, so that's what I did at Exmouth beach. I wasn't the only crazy man paddling in the sea as Wayne came too. The seawater can be great for any aches and pains. We had some team-building in the afternoon, with a barbecue at Roscoe D'Sane's house and Nicky Wroe on the case making some great food. He said that he gets it from his old man, so we must invite him down next time. It must have been one of the hottest days we've had for ages. I even managed to top up my tan. I really am a sun-worshipper and could sit in it all day. Hitting the sack early tonight as it's a road trip to Barrow tomorrow.

20/4/09 – Journey

Today's journey to play Barrow tomorrow has been the worst of the season, but with it being the most important game so far, we didn't mind. The match isn't going to be plain sailing by any means as they are fighting for their lives at the other end of the table. The whole journey took the best part of 8 hours, but it wasn't too bad, as we played about 100 games of cards, and for once I won a few. The other lads must have been more tired than me . . . which makes a change. Even though we had such a long journey we got off the bus, and went training straight away at Lancaster Football Club, just to get some of the stiffness out of us, and to work on our shape. Having trained there, it made me appreciate Plainmoor more than ever.

21/4/09 – Real Fans

It's the Barrow game today, but there's a bit of waiting around as it's an evening kick-off. The lads went off on their 'wish you were here' trip into Lancaster town centre for a walk, but it's not somewhere I'll be rushing back to. I went back to the hotel for an afternoon kip. We arrived at the ground to find the place bouncing, with the Barrow fans well up for it. But so were the Gulls fans, who had travelled in great numbers for the game. It really shows their loyalty to come all this way, especially considering it's a Tuesday – now that's what I call true football fans. We've been making things hard for ourselves lately and tonight's game was no exception. We drew 1–1, and no matter how hard we tried, we just couldn't get the winning goal. Now we have a truly must-win game against Burton at Plainmoor. We both need the win, so it should be a cracker. If we beat them and Cambridge win their match, then Burton could be the ones joining us in the play-offs. Football is a mad game, and you couldn't write an ending like this if you tried. I just pray that it's us who comes out on top.

22/4/09 – You Cannot Change the Past

We got back from the Barrow trip at 4.30 this morning so today has been one of those PJ days! It's been a day spent with Gemma and Amylia, but also about thinking of what might have been last night. You try not to dwell on things but it always plays on your mind. I'll have to try to forget yesterday and only think about tomorrow. You cannot change the past . . . you can only change the future.

23/4/09 – Haircut

A day off with the family today – Gemma, Amylia and Gemma's sister Lucie, were all out the back catching some rays. Later on I went to get the mop chopped, which hadn't been cut for some time. My super hairdresser Vanessa did it again. To be fair to her, she does have to work for her money. I even left a tip!

24/4/09 - Fate

It was very tense around the place today at training, with the big game coming up on Sunday. It's mad to think that you play 46 games in a league season, yet your fate can still come down to just one match. It's quite amazing to think that just a few years ago there was no play-off in the Conference, which meant that just one team got promoted to the Football League. Strange as it is I will never forget 2003 when I was with Exeter in the old English Third Division. We were the first team to get relegated as the team second from bottom. This meant that with two going down, two were promoted from the Conference. Going back to earlier days it must have been a nightmare for the fans. If you were in contention for the title at the top then your season could have been over at the halfway stage of the season, with nothing to play for – clear from the top, and clear from the bottom. That's not the case anymore since the Conference brought the play-offs into operation. The push for those four places can involve a whole host of teams for the duration of the season, and right into the last weekend. It's a second chance of some glory and another avenue to get promotion to the Football League. It can really turn up some stories and some great entertainment which is not for the faint-hearted. I just hope that this season we are one of those teams to get a second chance.

25/4/09 – Surprise in the Camp

Today is the day before we know where our fate will lie. We went in for a spot of training today, concentrating more on our shape than anything else. The gaffer announced the starting XI for the game, with only the one change from Tuesday night's game, and it was a bit of surprise, as Elliot Benyon got the nod ahead of Blair Sturrock. I really hope the young lad comes up trumps. This afternoon we went to watch Exeter play Morecambe in a big match in League Two. If Exeter had won they would have gone up automatically to League One. It's amazing to think that only a year ago we just missed out to them in the play-offs! Their match tonight ended 2–2, and they'll have to wait until the last game of the season to find out their fate . . . a bit like us really!

26/4/09 – Decision Day

Today was 'Decision Day'. We needed the win to carry us on into the play-offs, but knew that if we lost, and other teams won, then we'd slip out of contention.

It was the same old story, as we started poorly and went a goal down after 10 minutes. We managed to turn it around with a good team performance and what a decision by the gaffer to play Elliot, who scored the winner. The game was a bit surreal as Burton knew that they had the league won with 25 minutes left, but still battled on to try to win. The surreal feeling carried on after the ref had blown for full-time as both sets of supporters came onto the pitch to celebrate their respective teams' successes. Thank God the dream is still alive and kicking, and we're going to be playing Histon in a two-legged semi-final play-off. We're at home first, and then have to travel to their place four days later for the return leg. I'm happy we're playing at home first as the first time I ever played in a play-off we were at home first and got to the final. And let's not forget last year when we were away first but ended up losing over the two legs. I hope last year's history repeats itself, and we can stride forward to Wembley!

When I got home I went for a meal with my grandparents in Cullompton. What a great meal we had, and it was nice to spend time with them as they find it hard to get down as much as they used to.

27/4/09 - Jim'll Fix It

I had a lovely day today with my grandparents. We went for a walk in Tiverton and did a bit of shopping. It was a miserable day in terms of the weather, but it was really nice for my grandparents to spend time with Amylia. She loved it and called my grandmother 'Nan Nan' all day long. I bought a computer table, returned home quickly, and my grandfather and myself cracked on with putting it together. Every time he comes down we end up fixing or building something. He's a DIY God!

28/4/09 - Marathon Man

Today was the start of our training for the play-offs. We didn't do a lot, as there are still three days to go. You don't really want to do too much between now and the game, as you don't want to waste too much of your energy. After training I spent some time with my mate Barry McConnell, an ex-Exeter City player, who came around to tell me about his London Marathon run that he did on Saturday. Last year he did it in 3 hours flat, which is quite amazing, but this year was a disaster as he broke down after 8 miles with an injury. He then had to get the Tube, as he had to get his kitbag. Imagine the looks he got – people thought he was cheating! It's something I'd like to do one day . . . no, not break down after 8 miles, but to actually complete the race.

Speaking about running, I would like to give a special thanks to the supporters' marathon event organised by Matt Portt, Barry Middleton, Ken Stone and Julie Plumbridge. They took part in a run from Exeter's St James' Park to Plainmoor in Torquay, where they raised thousands of pounds for a cancer charity in honour of myself. I am very honoured to have received so much support. Everyone who took part can be very proud of themselves for what they achieved.

29/4/09 – Relaxed

I went to training as per usual today, and there was a really relaxed atmosphere around the place. That gives me a good feeling about Friday and let's hope it counts for something when we're playing.

Amylia had a bad day as she had her jab. I really feel for her, as she is also teething. It's heartbreaking that she can't tell us exactly what's wrong because she obviously can't talk yet. Luckily I was not home too late from training so I could give Gemma a break.

30/4/09 – Waiting

There's just one day to go now before the first leg. It was just short, sharp training today with plenty of ballwork.

Everyone has really been enjoying training this week in anticipation of the game. We watched the first leg of the other semi-final between Stevenage and Cambridge. What a game! Stevenage won 3–1, even though they had ten men for the whole of the second half. It's not over yet though, and there could be a few twists and turns in the second leg.

I hate to say it, but remember Exeter last season? They came from two behind in 10 minutes! That second-leg defeat was such a bitter pill to swallow. As you would guess, the Devon derbies are played in front of full houses. The first leg went to plan as we won 2–1 away from home at St James' Park. What a start it was, and obviously going into the second leg we had one foot on the bus to Wembley. In the return leg things got even better as we were 1–0 up with 20 minutes to go. I couldn't help thinking 'here we go again, off to the capital'. Big mistake, as it's not over until it's over, and Tisdale threw on a few forwards and completely changed Exeter's system. It was a tactical masterpiece from him and a real knife to the heart for me. They came back from a 3–1 aggregate score to win 4–3. Everything changed in 20 minutes. It was the worst feeling ever to have been ahead so comfortably, and then to throw it all away. Losing in a local derby is hard enough to take, but to lose to the team that I left last season (as captain) was soul-destroying. That's the play-offs for you.

1/5/09 – First Leg

Lots of sitting around today as kick-off isn't until 8.00 p.m. tonight. To get my mind off the game, we went shopping and then for some food in a really cheap Wetherspoons pub which is my dad's favourite, and it's becoming my favourite as well. Well to be fair, I need a good excuse to save money, as Gemma decided to spend £30 on a toy teddy for Amylia. Also, I hope we win tonight for the win bonus – haha!

It was a tough game but we stood up to Histon and played as a team. Once you do that, you're halfway there. We did what we had to do to match them, and once we had done that we let our quality shine through, as we won 2–0. We couldn't have wished for a better start in the play-offs, but it's still not over. We have to go and do the same in the away leg, but I know we're more than capable of doing that. It's not over until the fat lady sings . . . but I hope she's at least clearing her throat.

2/5/09 – Feeling Unwell

I woke up today feeling very dizzy and drained. I haven't felt like this before and thought that it must have been something to do with the way I got out of bed. I went in to training to do a warm down, but didn't feel any better so spoke to Damian, who decided that it would be best if I went to hospital for a check-up, just to make sure everything's fine with my blood. I got the results later and it was good news. I just need to take on more fluid, which is great. So when I got home I had a couple of glasses of water and went straight to bed. I didn't wake for the rest of the afternoon and it seemed to make the difference. Maybe I was just over-tired.

3/5/09 – Calm

We trained, and then travelled today, ready for the biggest game of the season, the second leg of the play-offs. These matches are always great for television, the players, and of course the supporters. It's the game that literally decides your whole season. The mood around the camp is chilled and very positive. The most important thing is that we're in the right frame of mind. We know it's not going to be easy, and that we will really have to fight for it. This time tomorrow we'll know our fate. I hope and pray that my dream is still alive, and kicking its way to England's home.

4/5/09 - Wembley, Here we Come!

It was a long day today waiting around for our destiny with a 5.00 p.m kick-off. I must say I was nervous, which I haven't been for quite some time when it comes to football. I think it's because of the hanging around we've done and seeing the result of the other game. As I told you, Stevenage were winning 3–1 after the first leg, but today they ended up losing 3–0, the victims of a last-minute goal in extra-time. That result showed that we still had a lot of work to do as our game was far from over. We knew that Histon wouldn't give up without a fight. Well, I wasn't wrong as we had a bad start and went 1–0 down after 16 minutes. I couldn't believe it, and felt sick with fear. They really took it to us, and we had to stay strong until half time to get in only one goal down. We settled a little in the second half and played better, with more of the play, and we managed to create a few half-chances. But it was one hell of a battle on a pitch which didn't even warrant being described as a farmer's field. We were still one down entering the last 10 minutes.

It was a nervy time, as another goal would have taken the game into extra-time. The Yellow Army and I were getting near to another Wembley trip. Hearts stopped with minutes left as, after another goalmouth scramble, a shot flew towards our goal, then from nowhere our keeper Pokey pulled off a super save, pushing the ball onto the bar and over to safety. After that I knew we were going to Wembley. It would be my third visit there. I found it so hard to control my emotions. All of those long, sleepless nights were well worth it.

We were going back, but most importantly, we were going back to win it. What a match. To top it all off I got the MOTM award. We had watched Cambridge celebrate in the morning after their victory, but this evening we remained calm and focused on the task ahead – winning promotion. We finished fourth in the league on 83 points. We were only 5 points off the top spot, having won 23, drawn 14 and lost 9 games. It had been very tight, though. There were seven teams battling for a place in the play-offs over the final few weeks of the season, and with only a few games to go any four of the group of Cambridge, Histon, Stevenage, Kidderminster, Oxford, Kettering or ourselves could have been in the play-offs. In fact we only finished 4 points ahead of sixth-placeed Kidderminster. Burton were worthy champions, but having lost Nigel Clough to Derby, their form was sketchy to say the least. Amazingly, when they found themselves 19 points clear in February, Conference sponsors Blue Square declared Burton the winners of the league and in a PR stunt and paid out all winning bets on them. Their lead was reduced week by week though, and as I said we were only 5 points behind them by the end of the season.

5/5/09 – Walking Home

It was some come-down this morning as we got back at about 2.00 a.m., and I had to walk home from where we got dropped off because Gemma was in bed and we only have the one car. Somehow I just can't picture John Terry walking home having played a game for Chelsea. . .

I woke up at around 11.00 with the biggest smile imaginable, thinking that the dream is still alive. The chance of playing League football again is within our grasp. We are off for a few days so I decided to go out for a few drinks with the lads to soak up what's gone on over the last few weeks. It was a nice day and it turned into a great night!

Having made it back to Wembley I got thinking back to when I was a second-year professional. I will never forget one Wednesday morning in particular. The full squad would always meet at the ground (the Vetch Field) and there would be the normal stuff going on; cups of tea, banter, and the weighing of every single player. It was to see how well you had been looking after yourself. It was no joke and was taken really seriously, well most of the time anyway, as one time when I was a YTS I made a right fool out of myself (again). I went into the warm room where we used to have the weighing scales as normal, but this time there were a few older pros in there (Matthew Bound, Julian Alsop, Ryan Casey and Kris O'Leary), finishing getting weighed. As a kid I was told that I needed to put on weight and it was something I tried so hard to do. I stood on the scales and to my amazement I couldn't believe it, I'd lost nearly 7 pounds, and was well gutted. When Ron Walton asked what I had been doing to have lost so much weight, the first thing that came into my head was that I had been spitting a lot. Well, I have never seen five grown men nearly brought to tears with laughter so easily. To this day I still can't believe I said that. I am quite often reminded of that day whenever I see my old Swans colleagues.

6/5/09 - Bank Details

I was a little rough around the edges today. When I finally got out of bed Gemma told me that we had received a letter from a jewellers in Milton Keynes. It said that someone had phoned them and tried to use my bankcard to buy jewellery under the name of Chris Todd. Later on I found out that whoever it was had managed to spend over £200 on two transactions. The only good thing is that they spent less than Gemma would have!

7/5/09 - Replay

I had another chilled-out day, did a bit of shopping and got some gardening stuff to fill the new pots my mum got me at a car boot sale. She really is the queen of the boot sales. Later I finally got around to watching the replay of the Histon game. It was hard to watch even though I knew the score. I try to watch the replays of as many matches I've played in as possible to try to look for both positive and negative aspects of my performance. If there are negatives then I make sure that I do my utmost not to make those mistakes again. I'm quite pleased, as I have managed to make 16 appearances for Torquay this season, scoring 1 goal. Here's a good one for you – I committed 26 fouls and didn't pick up a single booking!

8/5/09 - Wembley

We were back in training for the first time since the semi-final that took us to Wembley. It was good to be back. We had a chat about what we've done, and ultimately what we are going to do. We know that we still have a game to play.

Training was really sharp as all the lads were buzzing, and everyone is pushing really hard, because we all want a place in the squad. It was a long workout, which is what we needed, and after training the gaffer gave us some further time off, so we had the weekend to ourselves. I thought to myself that it would be the perfect time to go back to Wales to see the family. About an hour into the trip Gemma asked, 'Where are your tablets?' Disaster! I had forgotten them. So we rang the hospital and asked them if we could get some extra ones in Swansea, only to be told, 'not a chance'. The only thing we could do was go home, spoiling the weekend. Then I remembered that I had given some to my guardian angel Damian. I rang him and asked if he could send them express. He did, and saved the day. The man is a legend!

It doesn't surprise me that I have forgotten to take my tablets at times, as in truth, I'm a very forgetful person – always have been and always will be. I'd forget my head if it wasn't screwed on. When I was 16 years of age I was playing two years above my age with the Swansea City youths. I didn't drive at the time, so my parents drove me to the home games, which took place in the old Morfa Stadium where the Liberty Stadium stands today. On the way to a cup match I had a terrible feeling that I was missing something, but I couldn't muster up the courage to say it to my dad and was just praying that it was something non-essential, something that I could do without. We arrived at the ground, I got out of the car, opened the boot, looked through my bag and to my utter disbelief I had only forgotten to bring the footballer's essential tool – my boots! I couldn't believe it. My parents were still sitting in the car so I got back in and after a few seconds' pause I told them the story. All I'll say is thank God looks can't kill, as if they could, I wouldn't be sitting here writing this story today. The whole way back home in the car I got some telling-off. In the end we got back to the ground, and I was about 15 minutes late. There I got my second telling-off, this time from my manager Ron Walton, who told me that I was meant to be starting but was now on the bench. I was gutted about the telling-off but most of all I knew that I had blown my chance to start the match. On a positive note I got on for the last 20 minutes, and we won the game.

I will never forget that day for the rest of my life, and to this day I still get flashbacks of it. I guess it's ironic how as a kid I was nicknamed 'Rodney', after the character in *Only Fools and Horses*, for bearing a slight resemblance to him, and being a bit dull, but as the years went by I became known as 'Trigger'.

9/5/09 – Accident

We spent time with my brothers and their kids today. This is the first time the three cousins have spent time together. We went to a play zone where the kids had a blast. Then it all went horribly wrong when we went over to my mum's. We were in the living room having a cup of tea, when all of a sudden, like a flash, Amylia pulls mum's cup out of her hands. Then all you could hear was a scream. Well my heart sank. I couldn't believe what had just happened, but my mum picked her up as quick as lightning, took her to the tap and ran cold water over her arm. We didn't know how bad it was going to be, and I felt sick to think my little baby was hurt.

We went straight to A&E where they looked after her, but it still felt like a lifetime. They looked at it, and gave their opinion that they thought she would be fine, but to come in for a check-up tomorrow. When we got home Amylia was playing as if nothing had happened, but we were all in shock, especially my mum. I just hope that it will be fine tomorrow when we go back.

10/5/09 – Worried

We didn't sleep well last night, as both Gemma and myself were worried about today. Thank God we got the news we hoped for. They are only superficial burns that should heal fine on their own. A huge weight was lifted off our shoulders. We got back to my mum's and she was waiting at the door in a right mess, shaking like a leaf. It wasn't even her fault, and we told her that. It was an accident that could have happened to any of us, as we all had cups of tea in our hands.

We drove back to Devon tonight, ready to get back to training tomorrow.

11/5/09 – Good on you, KickBack

I received a nice letter this morning from a company called KickBack. I used them to claim back my overpaid tax money from the taxman, from expenses that I have paid over the past 6 years. Well, it was worthwhile doing, as there was a nice cheque attached. Also, had a good day in training where we worked hard defending as a unit.

12/5/09 – Think of the Fans

We had a full-scale practice match today and the lads looked very sharp, but we simply couldn't score, so I hope we're saving the goals for the weekend. We got four free tickets each, but I was hoping to get a few more, especially as the ground holds 90,000 and there will probably be around 40,000 there. Anyone who wants to get more has to pay the standard rate of £35. The tickets are too expensive in my book. It's shocking to make the fans have to pay that amount, and when they're getting them online they have to pay an extra £2. The League should remember it's also a big day for supporters!

13/5/09 – Trust Dinner

We had the day off today, so I just chilled out with the family. We were invited to the 'Legends' Dinner', held by the Torquay United Supporters' Trust. The trust was helping to raise money for leukaemia research, and have been a great support to me. I can't thank them enough for their support. Hopefully I can give something back to all those wonderful people by helping Torquay to a victory on Sunday, and get the club back to its rightful place in the Football League.

14/5/09 – Icing on the Cake

We started the first of a three-day training programme for the final. There was press everywhere, all looking for interviews. There must be a big game on soon or something . . . and yes, of course they wanted a few minutes with me – haha! The most common question related to how I felt going to Wembley considering all that had happened in the previous six months. I told them that it felt amazing, but the most important thing was to win. I just hope that all the work everyone has put in all season is rewarded on Sunday, and we get what we deserve. Let's not forget though, sometimes you don't always get what you deserve from life. This time I pray that we do. This will be my third time playing at Wembley in the past three seasons, and I hope it's third time lucky. It really would be the icing on the cake for me.

15/5/09 - Nervous

It's day two of our training camp today, and we are looking as sharp as ever. Instead of working on the defensive side of our game, we did the complete opposite and there were some great goals scored. Let's hope it carries through to Sunday. Only two days to go, and boy is the time going by quickly. The nerves are starting to kick in (slowly), and the more people talk about it, the more they tickle my belly!

16/5/09 - Last Training Session

All we had was a quick, sharp, training session today. When we were leaving on the team bus, there were hundreds of fans waiting to see us off. What a great sight, and I felt 10ft tall. On the bus we had the usual banter, played cards, and listened to some music. Greavsey, as was the norm, was winning, and I'd say he was on to Fiona, his missus, straight away telling her to buy some extra stuff in London, and not in Primark, but in Harrods on the strength of his winnings.

Thank God we only came to London the day before the match, as I would have been skint otherwise, while Greavsey would have been buying a new car. We got to our hotel in good time, so there was the opportunity for any of the squad who wanted to travel to Wembley and see the ground. Some of the lads went to see it, as they'd never been before, but it wasn't for me, as I wanted to treat the game as I would any other one. It's mad to think that we played the semi-final less than two weeks ago.

Tonight I tried to stay as relaxed as I possibly could and hopefully all I'll dream about is winning. Come this time tomorrow we will know our fate . . . and hopefully my dream will come true.

17/5/09 - Cannot Wait

I woke up early this morning at 7.30. I am blaming my room-mate, the skipper, who could not keep still with the excitement. To be honest, we were like two kids waiting to go on a school trip. But this was no school trip. It was the biggest game of my life, and I couldn't wait. I had a good feeling about it, and couldn't stop thinking about us lifting that trophy. We had the usual pre-match meal, and there was a nice mood around the place, but I could still feel a few nerves in the air too.

It felt surreal to be doing it all over again, for the third time, especially given what had gone on over the last six months. This was my third bus trip to Wembley, and for the gaffer too. You could say we are experienced travellers. But, if I'm being honest, my thoughts were on the last two years where it hurt so much to lose. Losing at Wembley is a terrible feeling, and I was praying that it wouldn't happen again.

There it was. Wembley. What a stadium. To think, a month ago we were playing in little Old Holker Street, in Barrow.

We were given a nice welcome from the fans, all dressed in yellow, who made themselves heard. All I can remember before the game was walking out the massive tunnel, out on to the pitch, and seeing the trophy sitting there, waiting for one team to claim it. This time it must be us.

Like every football fan I wanted to be a winner at Wembley. When it comes to big games you need big players. We had them today; the skipper who scored the first goal after 20 minutes, and Tim Sills who grabbed the second and all-important deciding goal in a 2–0 win. Today was about Torquay United FC. Every man played well in a Torquay shirt. The defence of Mansell, Nicolson and my central-defensive partner Robertson, who has come into his own over the last few months, were all as solid as rocks. We also have a wonderful goalkeeper in Michael Poke, who has been exceptional over the last few weeks. The midfield was well organised, and hardworking, with two flying wingers in Wayne and Danny. In the middle of the park we had Nicky Wroe and the skipper, the front-runners were a handful all game, and let's not forget the subs who came on. Also, I must mention the rest of the squad who have played their part in a long season. And finally, a big thank you to the management team who gave me my chance. I must however give a special mention to Scott Bevan because, before his injury, his form had been excellent.

When the referee blew the final whistle it was the best feeling ever. We're back in the Football League where we belong. After the game the celebrations were immense, both on and off the pitch. I felt in that half-hour that I let out all the bad stuff that had gone on in the past couple of months. The best feeling was when I saw my wife, my brothers and parents in the crowd looking so happy for me, and I think just a little bit proud.

But there was one thing that will live with me until the day I die, and that was hugging my dad as I came down the famous steps and seeing him with tears in his eyes. Both he and my mum were the happiest people alive and if there was anyone who deserved that happiness it was those two, after all they have seen in my career.

Later on it was nice getting so many 'well done' messages via text and also in person. I think we drank ourselves silly on the bus and sang all the way home. Today has been so special. It is something that will live with me all my life. For sure, my family and I will have a good summer knowing that we have done it. I have spent six long seasons battling to get back into the Football League, just missing out on the play-offs, losing in the semi-final, the final and now finally winning promotion.

When I was told I was ill, everything changed. I no longer worry about life's little problems. I don't take myself too seriously and try not to get uptight about things. I was laid-back before I got this illness but now I'd have to say I'm worse. I respect life much more now though, and really live each day as if it is my last.

To some, all that's happened would be so hard, but what I will say is that I believe that things happen for a reason in all walks of life, and today was just another chapter in a lifelong battle.

25/7/10 – Nerves

It's the night before the big fight and it's totally different to a night before a game of football where I'm just chilling out, only thinking of what I'm going to be watching on the box. This is different as I've got this really odd feeling in my stomach and can't get things off my mind – I suppose it's just nerves. I think it's the real facts I'm worried about, like being on my own in that ring. What if things aren't going my way? There's no-one to help me out in there. But I do know there will be someone there if I need help getting up off the canvas if I'm not careful.

The only thing that is the same is my food intake. I'm eating my normal night-before meal, good old Italian stallion chicken pasta. Hopefully I'll box like the real one (Rocky), you just never know. All I do know is that I'm as ready as I have ever been for a fight even if it's my first one!

I'm trying to take my mind off it all but I just can't. What happens if he makes me look a right chump in front of all my family and friends? Well at least I can say I got beaten by a cage fighter. The main thing is that there is a good turn-out, so we can make a lot of money for the charity!

26/7/10 – Charity Fight Night

It was the morning of the fight and you could say I should be resting, especially after last night where I didn't get much shut-eye. If you don't already know, us Todds don't do things by halves and make the most of every single day. Today was to be like no other. Gemma had decided to make the most of the Devon family coming down to Swansea and cram in a morning christening for our little princess Alanya. So it was off to the church for a very special moment, knowing that my smallest princess Alanya was to be christened just like Amylia. After the christening we all headed back for a small tea party at the Welcome Inn, Swansea, with all the family. Let's just say there were a few comments about my fight – apparently I had to watch I didn't get my arse kicked.

A few cups of tea and some cupcakes later, there was no rest for the wicked. Me and my brother Tom, who was also fighting in the show, had to go and get the

Penlan Social Club's main hall ready for the night. There was so much to do – banners, posters, etc. – to make the show work. The room layout had to be right. When we had finished prepping we then played the opening DVD film on the big screen that was donated by Leukaemia & Lymphoma Research. It brought a tear to my eye, and got me thinking about how lucky I really am and what I was about to achieve. We had put so much time and effort into this event and knew we were down to the finishing touches. The hall looked superb and made us so proud. It was time to head home to get some quiet time ahead of what was to come.

A few hours later it was time to get my bag ready and go. Out with the football boots and in with the gloves. Off I went in my little black Clio, tunes on, trying to get myself in the zone but all I could really think of was that I hoped people would turn up . . . and that I won my fight. A few top songs played and I arrived, got out the car and walked into the club. I felt like I was going to fight for a world title – the people's champion. The first people started to arrive, and of course it was all the other boxers and their families, all looking a bit nervous. The hall started to fill up and before long the place was buzzing with floods and floods of people. A great atmosphere began to build, and it looked like it was going to be a success. I was so relieved and knew then that I could concentrate on the fight.

We played the short film, which was a great start to the night as it made everyone understand the real reason we were there, not just for me but for the thousands and thousands of lives that had been saved through research. The mood was right and it was time for the fights. There were some tight battles on and the crowd loved every second of it. All I could do was anxiously watch and wait. The nerves were really jangling, but I couldn't wait.

The time arrived. My brother James had been doing all the boxers' corners for the red side, and came in to get me. We walked down the corridor, people wishing me well. We waited outside the doors to the hall, and I took a cheeky look inside. The people were buzzing. I wanted to go in but James wouldn't let me until the time was right. The music was blaring, the crowd was going wild but still James wouldn't let me go in. 'Wait until the music really kicks in,' he said.

With that a roar of 'Toddy! Toddy! Toddy!' came blaring out. My heart was racing and the hairs on the back of my neck stood up. Then it was time, 'Let's go, bro.'

I walked through the doors and felt I was on a different planet. The crowd was going crazy. I got to the side of the ring, and James stopped me. He said, 'Calm down. You have not come all this way to lose this fight. Now get in there and win.' Well that was the last thing I remember. I got in, ducked, weaved, punched, and fought like I had never fought before, doing things I never knew I had in my locker. Round by round I grew in confidence, and yes, I took some sweet hooks for my sins (God, he could hit hard). My jaw felt like it was on someone else's head at times. But every time he hit me I went straight back for more, chucking in three and four combos.

The fight finished and the crowd got louder and louder. Cheers erupted but all I could think was 'wow, thank God that's over'. I gave my opponent Craig 'Bunny' Allen a hug. Then they announced the winner. I felt I had done enough to win and yes, I did. I was buzzing, as was everyone else. The night was a great success and we raised over £3,000 for the charity in what was a very special event. After getting a stiff jaw, I was well overdue for a stiff pint. Cheers!

Epilogue

I am now in a full state of remission which means my blood is showing very little, if any, sign of the leukaemia cells. I cant believe I'm quickly approaching my third year in remission and my fourth year since that dreaded day of being told. One thing is for sure, I have lived every day to the max, and I am so grateful to have a second chance in life.

In 2010 I left Torquay United and signed for Newport County, uprooting back to Swansea. Moving house is something everybody knows is a stressful and no-one knows this more than my wife Gemma, as for the first time in twenty-six years I helped her pack her bags and leave stunning Devon. We stayed in Wales for two and a half years, spending quality time with my family.

People will wonder why I left Torquay. It was simply about two friends not seeing eye-to-eye, and deciding to close the door on something that was good, but had over-run. I'm not a bitter man. I fell in love with a club, but I felt that I had a lot more to offer and parted for the good of my career and wish Torquay and the staff every success. I'm sure one day down the line our paths will cross again.

After leaving one success at Torquay I joined another in the colour of orange, a kit colour I always wanted to play in as I used to love watching Holland as a kid. Newport is a sleeping giant, and I hoped that I could play a big part in helping them wake up. I felt that I had been there for years, having won the Blue Square Conference South in unbelievable fashion, breaking all sorts of records. Who would of thought I could be so successful in such a short space of time?

To say that the first year in the Blue Square Premier was a success would be an understatement. To take to the league like we did was remarkable and halfway through the season we were sitting in the top half of the table and looking like strong play-off contenders.

Then a bombshell hit as the gaffer Dean Holdsworth took over at Aldershot. After he left things went pear-shaped; he had been such a big part of what had happened at Newport. The bond he had with the players was unique and when he departed it left so many players in disbelief – it was the sucker-punch of our season. We went on a run that left a lot to be desired and were nowhere near where we were earlier in the season.

I still believe to this day that if the club had made a swift decision on a new manager, we would have made the play-offs. But it was not to be, and it wasn't until two months before the season ended that Anthony Hudson came in and we ended up finishing in tenth position. It was a case of what might have been.

I was getting ready for my second season with Newport as I had previously signed a two-year deal when I got the strangest of calls from Tim Harris to say that if I didn't stick pen to paper for my second year, then my contract didn't exist. It was a shock to say the least! I knew I had the second year, and that there were a few things that needed to be sorted as the club were going full-time. I didn't know that I had the option to leave but that was the case. I believed that I needed to get a few extra pennies to cover my travelling costs for the extra days but that never really materialised. It became a game of cat and mouse, and left me doubting what the club really wanted. In the end I got so many mixed signals that I began speaking to other clubs including Wrexham, Darlington, Bath and Forest Green Rovers.

Having spoken to these clubs I weighed up my options, and decided to join the club I nearly joined twelve months earlier, namely David Hockaday's Forest Green Army. It ticked all the right boxes and really appealed to me in so many different ways. By the time I had agreed to sign with them I received a text from Newport with the offer I had been waiting to hear from the very start.

It was too late in the day, though – I had already committed my heart to Forest Green Rovers. I loved my time at Newport County and cannot thank the club and fans enough.

As you may have guessed, after signing for FGR my yo-yo family were on the move again, leaving Swansea to head back down to Devon, where I currently commute back and forth from Stroud. Since joining Forest Green Rovers my career and health took another halt, though this time it was not because of the leukaemia. With a great pre-season under my belt I was raring to go, playing in the first game of the season against Stockport live on Premier Sports TV. However, 60 minutes into the game I found myself overstretching my hamstring and pulling it of the bone. I sustained an avulsion fracture, that left me needing surgery and it kept me out for seven months. The rehab was, to say the least, character-building.

I soon become a fan of Forest Green Rovers rather than a player, in a season where my nails took a hammering. With a month or so of the season left, I got myself back in contention thanks to the help of the football club and physio Tim Grigg. It was not long after the gaffer gave me my first-team return against Telford in the Blue Square Premier.

By now you will know there is always a story in Chris Todd's life and seventeen minutes into my return I put in a over eager tackle that saw me red-carded. I can only put it down to six months of frustration but I left the pitch in utter disbelief. I got suspended for three games and sat out the remainder of the season. In that period of being injured and suspended, I put my spare time to good use and found myself working hard on my book doing a lot of publicity.

In the last year I have had some incredible news as my wife is expecting our third child in September 2012, and this time it's a boy. Adding a son to my two special girls and my incredible wife makes me feel complete.

I look forward to the future and my career – the future bright, the future Green.

Postscript

In 2002 Chris signed a short-term contract with my local League of Ireland club Drogheda United. He was here for a little under a season, but left a lasting impression and achieved cult hero status due to his performances at centre-back. Chris subsequently moved back to Britain, signing for Exeter. Since then he has carved out an exceptional career for himself at Torquay, Salisbury, Newport and now Forest Green.

I interviewed Chris for *DUFC: A Claret and Blue History*, an anecdotal account of Drogheda United's history. While doing this in 2008, I received the news that Chris had been diagnosed with leukaemia, and like all football fans, I was shocked.

Chris asked me to come on board with this book in January 2011. I'll never forget the first time I set Chris 'homework' – a list of questions for him to answer in order to fix up the book. He laughed at the suggestion but within a few hours he was working hard on the team bus, and I had received my answers.

This book is a deeply personal, honest and frank account of a leukaemia sufferer's battle with this life-threatening illness. At times it's not for the faint of heart. One thing that you will notice is that Chris never looks for sympathy from anyone – instead he wishes to inspire.

You can feel his determination to get back playing again, and will him on. We are all included in his journey; there's more to this book than just football and this, for me, is where the true story lies. Chris talks honestly about his relationship with his wife Gemma and children, the other members of his family, and how everybody coped during his illness.

They say football is a game of two halves. So is life.

Brian Whelan, 2012